Spiritual leaders acclaim *The Prayer-Shaped Disciple*

THE PRAYER-SHAPED DISCIPLE is so full of practical insight into the purpose and power of prayer that I consider it one of the most important books on this vital subject published in recent years. Dan Crawford takes us well beyond Prayer 101 to a graduate level encounter in what it means to be a prayer-shaped disciple of Jesus.

—Dr. Dick Eastman
International President
Every Home for Christ

THIS IS ONE of those books that comes along every so often that will speak to you no matter where you are spiritually. If your prayer life is weak or if you pray like Daniel, there is something here for you that will deeply effect your relationship with the Heavenly Father. Read and be blessed—I was.

—Dale Schlafer
Vice President for Revival and Awakening
PromiseKeepers

DAN CRAWFORD WRITES not as a theoretician but as one who knows what it is to be on his knees. This book not only will give you practical instruction for prayer, it will inspire you to pray. I recommend the book with enthusiasm.

—Dr. Timothy Beougher
Billy Graham Associate Professor of Evangelism
The Southern Baptist Theological Seminary
Louisville, Kentucky

THIS BOOK IS filled with practical help, not pious platitudes. If you are serious about developing your prayer life, this is a great place to start.

—Rick Warren
Senior Pastor, Saddleback Valley Community Church
Author, *The Purpose-Driven Church*

IN THIS DAY of impending revival, in the midst of an unprecedented movement of united prayer, nothing could be more important than teaching God's people how prayer and discipleship synergize. Dan Crawford has given us extremely practical insights on this. Thousands are ready to learn, and poised to obey.

—David Bryant
Founder and President
Concerts of Prayer International

THE PRAYER-SHAPED DISCIPLE is instructive, inspiring, and practical—all the ingredients necessary to shape you into a disciple who impacts his world through prayer.

—Alice Patterson
Prayer Texas

ANY PERSON WHO desires to be an authentic and effective disciple of Jesus Christ can benefit from this book. Dan Crawford not only contends that the life of prayer is central to discipleship, he teaches us how to make it central.

—Paul Cedar
Chairman
Mission America

IN A TIME when many Christian leaders speak about a new mission paradigm and a world wide awakening, *The Prayer-Shaped Disciple* will be a welcomed work in helping us form a biblical foundation for what is happening. Crawford has drawn on his own experiences as well as those of others to give us a solid, practical book dealing with both prayer and discipleship.

—Dr. Bill Wagner
E. Harmond Westmareland Professor of Evangelism
Golden Gate Baptist Theological Seminary

A WONDERFUL STUDY, filled with practical insight to God-initiated prayer. Reading this book opens the windows of heaven.

—Dr. Robert E. Coleman
Director of the School of World Mission and Evangelism
Trinity International University

MY SPIRITUAL LIFE was enriched, and my prayer life deepened and expanded as I read Dr. Dan Crawford's book *The Prayer-Shaped Disciple*....This book reveals how prayer is the heartbeat of all that we do in worship, ministry, and evangelism. It is the golden chair that links heaven and earth together.... *The Prayer-Shaped Disciple* has blessed me beyond measure. I believe it will be a blessing to anyone who reads it.

—Dr. Jack Stanton
Founder/Director Emeritus of the Institute of Evangelism
Southwest Baptist University
President & Director, Jack Stanton World Evangelism Association

IN THE SELF-ABSORPTION of our pragmatic present, prayer is so often just a technical attempt to shape God's responses into the image of our own desires. How refreshing to find a volume that rightly holds forth the truth, in comprehensive fashion, that prayer is the natural and irresistible hunger of every believer for fellowship with God and that in it we find the Master Potter shaping us and our requests into the image of His great desires.

—Dr. Randy Sprinkle
Director, International Prayer Strategy Office
International Mission Board, Southern Baptist Convention

DR. CRAWFORD COVERS every aspect of prayer, and in an informative, biblical, challenging and practical way. I can honestly say it is an excellent work. If all God's people would immerse themselves in this volume, revival—personal and corporate—could come.

—Dr. Lewis A. Drummond
Billy Graham Professor of Evangelism and Church Growth
Beeson Divinity School

DAN CRAWFORD IS no stranger to prayer in his personal life. What a wonderful, practical, encouraging book! Read it, and get to know better the God who made you.

—Alvin L. Reid
Associate Professor of Evangelism and Church Growth
Bailey Smith Chair of Evangelism
Southeastern Baptist Theological Seminary

DAN CRAWFORD DEMONSTRATES his passion for prayer through this practical, inspirational and well-researched new book. I know it will encourage all who read it.

—Richard Blackaby
President, Canadian Southern Baptist Seminary

PRAYER IN THE Bible. Prayer in history. Prayer methods. Prayer language. Just about everything you need to know about prayer. Dan Crawford weaves a wealth of information and insights with stories, scripture and structure to help Christians become prayer-shaped disciples. From the prayer novice to the prayer warrior, here is your handbook on prayer.

—Leith Anderson
Wooddale Church
Eden Prairie, Minnesota

THE PRAYER-SHAPED DISCIPLE is a "seminary course" on prayer; a reference book; a gold-mine of inspirational and practical helps for those who would invest themselves in prayer. I recommend it highly and will refer to it again and again!

—Eddie Smith
U. S. Prayer Track

THE PRAYER-SHAPED DISCIPLE is a rare but extremely helpful blend of strong Biblical exposition, inspiring illustrations, and insightful suggestions on the necessity of, as well as the art of, effective praying. Any Christian will benefit from reading and re-reading this book. I recommend it enthusiastically.

—Larry L. Lewis
National Facilitator for Celebrate Jesus 2000
Mission America

THE PRAYER-SHAPED DISCIPLE is an amazing prayer resource of scriptures, word studies, pertinent information, and inspiring illustrations.... Rarely have I seen such a comprehensive treatment of prayer in all of its biblical aspects. I highly recommend this book to everyone serious about God and one's daily walk with Christ.

—Minette Drumwright
Retired Director, International Prayer Strategy Office
International Mission Board, Southern Baptist Convention

THE WORD *IMPRESSED* expresses my feelings toward *The Prayer-Shaped Disciple*. I was impressed with Dan Crawford's constant use of scripture, fertile use of illustrations, constant use of variety, expansive use of bibliography, and lively use of the Lord's model. To all who pick up this book, I say, "Go for it!"

—Don Miller
Director
Bible Based Ministries

The Prayer-Shaped Disciple

The Prayer-Shaped Disciple

Learn How Prayer Can Enrich Your Spiritual Life

Dan R. Crawford

The Prayer-Shaped Disciple
©1999 by Dan R. Crawford
Published by Hendrickson Publishers, Inc.
P.O. Box 3473
Peabody, Massachusetts 01961-3473

Unless otherwise noted, all scripture is from the New American Standard Bible, ©1960, 1962, 1963, 1968, 1971, 1972, 1973, 1975, 1977, 1995 by the Lockman Foundation. La Habra, California. Used by permission.

Portions of the author's earlier book on prayer, *Connecting with God*, are used by permission.

Printed in the United States of America

ISBN 1-56563-092-0

First printing—March 1999

Cover design by Veldheer Creative Services, Byron Center, Mich.
Interior design by Pilcrow Book Services, Kirkland, Wash.
Edited by Judy Bodmer, Geoff Pope, and Heather Stroobosscher

To Danna and James

Objects of My Prayers
Since Their Births

and

To My Prayer Warriors

Always laboring earnestly ... in ... prayers.
Colossians 4:12

Contents

Introduction

While visiting with a group of friends, the subject was raised of my recent prayer journeys through parts of China, India, and the Middle East. In the course of the conversation the word "prayerwalking" was used. This is a popular term relating to praying on site with new insight. Contrary to what may seem obvious, it is not limited to walking. Often those praying will ride in cars or taxi cabs, on buses, trains, or boats, or even on bicycles. Frequently they will be in meetings with religious leaders, praying as they are informed of concerns. However, another friend, who frequently takes things too literally, exclaimed, "Wow! If you walked across all those countries, you must be in great physical shape." Then a more contemplative member of the group entered the conversation with this thought: "He may not be in great physical shape, but he is prayer-shaped."

It was the second time I had heard that phrase, "prayer-shaped." As I was working on this manuscript, my previous book, *Discipleshape: Twelve Weeks to Spiritual Fitness*, was released. It discusses personal spiritual disciplines, including prayer. I was trying to discover a title for this work on prayer that somehow connected back to the idea of spiritual fitness. My father suggested the idea of being a prayer-shaped disciple. I thought of the other spiritual disciplines. I could be a witness-shaped disciple, a giving-shaped disciple, a service-shaped disciple, or a worship-shaped disciple. While I desired to be all of those, I really wanted to be a prayer-shaped disciple. To me, prayer is the priority among spiritual disciplines. The idea lodged in my mind and I had a book title.

You and I have a basic need to communicate with God. But where does this need come from? The Bible tells us that we, male and female, are created in the image of God (Gen. 1:27) and that God breathed into us "the breath of life; and man became a living being" (Gen. 2:7). Sometime during the sixth day of creation, God had completed all the work except for one act. As yet, nothing had been made in God's own image. So, as God's climactic act, humankind was shaped in the image of God. Designed in his image, we were made for the purpose of communion with God.

Very simply defined, prayer is two-way communication with God. You and I were made in God's image for relationship with God and when we became followers of Jesus Christ, we began a process of becoming prayer-shaped disciples. Could it be that God desires to have fellowship with us and that our need to commune with God is a result of God's greater need to commune with us? Could it be that God shaped us for this very purpose?

Let us remember communication is a priority, and God is the subject of our priority. We must understand the proper source of power in prayer. Contrary to almost everything written about it, prayer is not the most powerful force in the world. God is. More things have not been wrought by prayer than this world dreams of. More things have been wrought *by God in response to faith expressed* through prayer than this world has dared to dream. The idea set forth in this book is that all prayer begins with God and progresses as we communicate with God. An unknown author wrote:

> I sought the Lord, and afterward I knew
> He moved my soul to seek Him, seeking me;
> It was not I that found, O Savior true,
> No, I was found of Thee.

Communication with God must be a priority of the Christian life as it was for the disciples of our Lord. According to Luke's account of the Gospel, the disciples were confronted by many things between the time Jesus called them to follow him (Luke 5:1ff) and the time they asked him to teach them to pray (Luke 11:1). The disciples were confronted by many issues (see sidebar). Yet, after all of this, they recognized the priority of prayer. They did not ask to be taught how to heal illness, to exorcise demons, to raise the dead, to settle opposition, to teach, to relate, to meet physical needs, to understand their own call, to fulfill their mission, or to answer tough questions. They asked Jesus to teach them to pray. Prayer was his Father's idea and the priority for Jesus' disciples. These men were to be prayer-shaped.

The thought that prayer is God's idea and not ours and that prayer means more to God than it does to us is foreign to most believers. We operate on the assumption that prayer is our idea and that communication with God is initiated by us in our times of need. That assumption leads us to believe that when we pray we have to get God's attention and hold it by using the right terminology. Underneath that assumption is

---

Issues the Disciples Confronted:

- Human illness (Luke 5:12–16, 17–26; 7:1–10, 8:41–48)
- Demon possession (Luke 8:26–39; 9:37–45)
- Death (Luke 7:11–17; 8:40–42, 49–56)
- Opposition (Luke 9:51–56)
- New teaching (Luke 6:17–49; 8:1–18; 9:57–62; 10:25–37)
- Relationships (Luke 6:12–16; 7:18–50, 8:19–21; 9:28–36; 10:38–42)
- Physical needs (Luke 8:22–25; 9:10–17)
- Their own call (Luke 5:1–11, 27–32; 6:12–16)
- Their mission (Luke 9:1–6; 10:1–24)
- Questions (Luke 5:33–39; 6:1–11; 9:18–27; 9:46–50)

the belief that we must live the right kind of life to be worthy of communication with God. Prayer then becomes a heavy burden. We become hesitant to pray because of our lifestyle or our lack of knowing the right words.

Yet, in prayer we are offered the high privilege of communication with God. Prayer is intended to be divine sharing on matters of importance to God. We are invited to deliberate at a celestial board meeting, to participate in a summit meeting in the oval office of the universe.

At the outset of this book, let me offer a word about format and content. Even as I write I have asked myself, why another book on prayer? There are so many already available on the subject that we could well spend our lives studying prayer and never do much of it. So I am faced with the tension of whether I should offer more information or leave this unwritten and encourage more time for doing it. In the hours you will spend reading this book, you could actually have spent precious minutes in the presence of God. Still, I hope these pages will teach you the value of time spent communicating with God and assist you in having a life shaped by prayer. I pray that the time you give this book will complement the time you spend in actual prayer and the result will be a *prayer-shaped disciple.*

Acknowledgments

Special thanks go to Jan Brown, Helen Hanson, Madonna Krebs, and Beth Cochran for their many hours working with the manuscript. Significant ideas in this book were inspired by students in my weekly prayer and accountability groups and classes on prayer at Southwestern Baptist Theological Seminary, Northeastern Baptist School of Ministry, Canadian Southern Baptist Seminary, and Hong Kong Baptist Theological Seminary. My sincere thanks to all these students, but especially the following prayer and accountability group members spanning the years: Jack Allen, Steve Allen, Darrell Blaine, Calvin Bone, Lance Borden, Derek Boyd, Jim Bricker, Jason Browning, Conley Bush, Erik Carlsen, Darrell Carnley, Mike Chadwick, Tom Clemmons, Scott Coleman, Scott Corwin, John Cross, Sam Day, Shane Evett, Terry Fields, Jeff Glenn, Rick Griffin, Bailey Harris, Len Hedgecock, Jerry Hofmeister, Mike Hoyt, Gene Jennings, John Littleford, Paul Mastin, Donald McLachlan, John Morse, Brian Mott, Steve Murray, Craig O'Brien, Phil Porter, Scott Rambo, Charlie Sherrod, Gary Smith, Kevin Steele, Jeff Thompson, Roy Thompson, Steve Warr, Mike Warthen, Tony Wilford, Kevin Wirt, Blake Withers, and Bob Wood.

PART ONE

The

Prayer-Shaped

Disciple

Prays

With

While witnessing to a young Jewish man, Alfred Ackley was asked, "Why should I worship a dead Jew?" Ackley immediately responded, "He lives!" Later, reflecting on this conversation, Ackley wrote:

> He lives, He lives,
> Christ Jesus lives today!
> He walks with me and talks with me
> Along life's narrow way.

Because Jesus Christ lives, all communication barriers between God and humankind are destroyed. Through Jesus, we are enabled to enter into two-way communication with God. The key to understanding prayer as communication is the word "with." In prayer we communicate *with* God and God communicates *with* us.

In March 1912, C. Austin Miles was reading John 20, his favorite chapter in the Bible. Concerning his experience he wrote:

> As I read it that day, I seemed to be part of the scene. I became a silent witness to that dramatic moment in Mary's life, when she knelt before her Lord and cried, "Rabboni!"

My hands were resting on the Bible while I stared at the light blue wall. As the light faded I seemed to be standing at the entrance of a garden, looking down a gently winding path, shaded by olive branches. A woman in white, with head bowed, hand clasping her throat, as if to choke back her sobs, walked slowly into the shadows. It was Mary. As she came to the tomb, upon which she placed her hand, she bent over to look in, and hurried away.

John, in flowing robe, appeared, looking at the tomb; then came Peter, who entered the tomb, followed slowly by John.

As they departed, Mary reappeared; leaning her head upon her arm at the tomb, she wept. Turning herself, she saw Jesus standing; so did I. I knew it was he. She knelt before him with arms outstretched and looking into his face, she cried, "Rabboni!"

I awaked in full light, gripping the Bible, with muscles tense and nerves vibrating. Under the inspiration of this vision I wrote as quickly as the words would be formed the poem exactly as it has since appeared. That same evening I wrote the music.[1]

The poem written and set to music that day was the beloved hymn "In the Garden:"

> And He walks with me, and He talks *with* me,
> And He tells me I am His own,
> And the joy we share as we tarry there,
> None other has ever known. (Italics mine)

Not only does God *walk with* us, God also *talks with* us. What a blessing to know that in the midst of life God is indeed *with* us. At the beginning, then, let us consider the fact that the prayer-shaped disciple prays *with*. As we're about to discover, he or she prays:

- with heavenly prayer partners
- with earthly prayer partners
- with awareness of God's responses
- with basic ingredients
- with privacy
- with the Lord's Prayer

1. Heavenly Prayer Partners:
Connecting with Heaven

Little words often carry the weight of a thought. In fact, prepositions are extremely important in the transmission of ideas—perhaps never more so than when related to our heavenly prayer partners. Consider the prepositions *to, in, with,* and *through.*

The Bible teaches that we should pray *to* the Father. Matthew 6:6 says, "When you pray ... pray to your Father." Matthew 6:9 says, "Pray, then, in this way:'Our Father who is in heaven'." John 16:23 says, "If you ask the Father for anything in My name, He will give it to you." When you call upon the Father, do you realize what kind of father he is? We call not on a father who is preoccupied with his career and has little time for his children. We call not on a father who may find someone else he loves more and so forsake us. Nor does the father on whom we call simply cater to our whims while we manipulate him. Our heavenly Father is not weak and passive, nor is he unable to make decisions. He is available always. In my hymntext *Call Upon the Father,* I wrote:

We must call upon the Father,
    Praying that His Will be done,
With the Spirit interceding
    In the name of God's own Son.
We will humbly bow before Him
    Yet come boldly to His throne;
Praise His mighty name forever
    And adore Him as our own.

God will answer those who ask Him;
    Seeking Him will help us find.
Those who knock will find Him open
    To our heart, our soul, our mind.
We do not know what He'll show us,
    Great and mighty things they are,
But we know that he will answer
    Every call from near and far.

Then some day we'll stand before Him;
    In His presence we'll abide.
He will talk with us forever,
    As we walk close by His side.
Calling here upon the Father
    Will our daily manna be,
Calling there upon the Father
    Abba for eternity.

We are to pray *to* and *in* the name of Jesus. How frequently the Bible teaches this:

- John 14:13-14 says, "Whatever you ask in My name, that will I do, so that the Father may be glorified in the Son. If you ask Me anything in My name, I will do it."
- Romans 8:34 says, "Christ Jesus is He who died, yes, rather who was raised, who is at the right hand of God, who also intercedes for us."
- John 15:16 says, "You did not choose Me but I chose you, and appointed you that you would go and bear fruit, and that your fruit would remain, so that whatever you ask of the Father in My name He may give to you."

- Romans 10:12 says, "There is no distinction between Jew and Greek; for the same Lord is Lord of all, abounding in riches for all who call on Him."
- 2 Corinthians 12:8 says, "Concerning this I implored the Lord three times that it might leave me."

The New Testament affirms prayer addressed to the Son as well as to the Father. "Lord" is the covenant name of God in the Greek Old Testament but changes in the New Testament. The expression "calling upon the name of the Lord" appears often in Acts and in the letters of the New Testament. Always it is a reference to calling upon Christ as Lord. Only Stephen directs a prayer specifically to "Jesus" and then the address is "Lord Jesus" (Acts 7:59-60).

Praying *in* the name of Jesus or *in* the name of the Lord is only proper when the prayer reflects the will and purpose of the Lord. One cannot pray in his name without also praying for his sake or according to his will. Prayers that conclude with the words "*in* the Name of Jesus," but that do not reflect the will of Jesus will not be honored.

Praying *in* the name of Jesus also implies praying to the names of Jesus. The psalmist says: "And those who know Thy name will put their trust in Thee; for Thou, O LORD, have not forsaken those who seek Thee" (Ps. 9:10). As specific occasions arise one might call upon the Lord by some name specifically related to that circumstance. In times of illness, one might pray to the Great Physician (Matt. 9:9-13; Mark 2:14-17; Luke 5:27-32). In times of spiritual darkness, one might pray to the Light (John 8:12; 9:5; 12:46). In times of loneliness or distress, one might pray to the Friend (Matt. 11:19; Luke 7:34; John 15:13).

Dick Eastman and Jack Hayford state in their book *Living and Praying in Jesus Name*, "Christ extended to His disciples a certain 'power of attorney'—the authority to use His name in transacting business on His behalf."[1] They then write thirty-one chapters (one for each day of the month), each focusing on a different name (see table on next page).

One specific example of calling on a name related to Jesus is found in the life of Joseph Scriven for whom Jesus was a treasured friend. On October 10, 1886, the lifeless body of Joseph Scriven was pulled from Lake Rice in Canada. He was sixty-six years old and had been one of the most beloved citizens of the town, especially by the poor. When he was young, he had been engaged to a beautiful girl in Ireland. The day before the wedding, she was tragically drowned. Scriven migrated to Canada to forget. Ten years later his mother fell ill of grief over him. He wrote the following poem to her:

> What a friend we have in Jesus
> All our sins and griefs to bear!
> What a privilege to carry
> Everything to God in prayer!

Some scriptural names for Christ:

A Wall of Fire (Zech. 2:5)	The Lord Who Heals (Exod. 15:26)
A Sure Foundation (Isa. 28:16)	The Bridegroom (Matt. 25:10)
A Refiner and Purifier (Mal. 3:3)	Wonderful Counselor (Isa. 9:6)
A Nail Fastened in a Sure Place (Isa. 22:23)	The Cornerstone (Ps. 118:22)
A Great Light (Isa. 9:2)	The Lifter of My Head (Ps. 3:3)
A Scepter (Num. 24:16–17)	My Rock (Ps. 31:3)
A Quickening Spirit (1 Cor. 15:45)	The Power of God (1 Cor. 1:24)
The Head of the Body (Col. 1:18)	The Wisdom of God (1 Cor. 1:24)
The Lord of Peace (2 Thess. 3:16)	The Way, The Truth and The Life (John 14:6)
The Brightness of His Glory (Heb. 1:3)	The Deliverer (Rom. 11:26)
The Express Image of His Person (Heb. 1:3)	The Lord of Glory (1 Cor. 2:7–8)
The Propitiation of Our Sins (1 John 2:2)	The Bread of Life (John 6:35)
The Hidden Manna (Rev. 2:17)	The Bright and Morning Star (Rev. 22:16)
The Amen (Rev. 3:14)	The Word of God (Rev. 19:13)
The Lion of the Tribe of Judah (Rev. 5:5)	The Captain of the Hosts of the Lord
The Alpha and Omega (Rev. 1:8)	(Josh. 5:14)

Oh, what peace we often forfeit
Oh what needless pain we bear,
All because we do not carry
Everything to God in prayer!

Have we trials and temptations?
Is there trouble anywhere?
We should never be discouraged
Take it to the Lord in prayer:
Can we find a friend so faithful
Who will all our sorrows share?
Jesus knows our every weakness
Take it to the Lord in prayer.

Are we weak and heavy laden
Cumbered with a load of care?
Precious Savior, still our refuge
Take it to the Lord in prayer.
Do thy friends despise, forsake thee?
Take it to the Lord in prayer;
In his arms He'll take and shield thee
Thou will find a solace there.

Concerning the use of the names of Jesus in times of prayer, Alexander Maclaren wrote these profound words:

I think of His names, I trust in them, I present them to Him whom they all but partially declare; and I ask Him—for His own name's sake, because of what He is and hath declared Himself to be—to hear my poor cry, to answer my imperfect faith, to show Himself yet once again that which His name has from of old proclaimed Him to be.

For us to know and trust that name is the highest exercise of all faith. To utter it believing is the very essence of all true prayer. Not as a formal beginning and as a formal close, but as the only ground of acceptance, do we connect it with our petitions. It should begin our prayers as their foundation; it should end them as their seal.

The bare utterance of a name may be the purest formalism, or it may be the most intense faith. The deepest love often finds that all language fails and that to breathe the beloved name is enough. All tenderness may be put in it—all rapture, all praise.[2]

As our heavenly prayer partner, Jesus prays for us just as he did for his disciples (Luke 22:32; John 17; Rom. 8:34; Heb. 7:25; Heb. 9:24; 1 John 2:1). As a prayer partner, Jesus affects our own prayer life in at least three ways: we learn to pray in agreement with him, in confidence with him, and in persistence with him. Jesus prays within our prayers, and his prayer is answered on our behalf. The New Testament tells us that when our prayer is "only a groan or a sob, Christ takes the sob on His own lips; and God, knowing which is our sob and which is Christ's, answers us for Christ's sake, and Christ for our sake."[3]

Addressing the fact that Jesus is always interceding for us, Carolyn Gilman writes:

> And He's ever interceding
> To the Father for His children
> Yes, He's ever interceding
> To the Father for His own
> Through Him you can reach the Father
> So bring Him all your heavy burdens
> Yes, for you He's interceding
> So come boldly to the throne.[4]

We should pray *with, in,* and *through* the Holy Spirit. The role of the Holy Spirit in prayer is described by Paul in these words: "We do not know how to pray as we should, but the Spirit Himself intercedes for us with groanings too deep for words; and He who searches the hearts knows what the mind of the Spirit is, because He intercedes for the saints according to the will of God" (Rom. 8:26–27). When our situation is so intense that we cannot even verbalize our petitions to God, the Holy Spirit takes over and "intercedes for us." Thus, the Holy Spirit also acts as a prayer partner, first entering into us when we become a believer and then indwelling us more fully through prayer. According to Romans 8:26–27, the Holy Spirit "helps our weakness," guides us in "how to pray as we should," "intercedes for us," "searches the hearts," and helps us discern "the will of God."

Concerning prayer and its relationship to the Holy Spirit, Paul Y. Cho, pastor of the largest church in Korea, confesses, "Every major principle that I teach in Korea and around the world did not come from a theological book, but it came from genuine and intimate fellowship with the Holy Spirit in prayer."[5]

The Apostle Paul further describes the role of the Holy Spirit in prayer by writing, "With all prayer and petition pray at all times in the Spirit" (Eph. 6:18). Jude writes, "You, beloved, building yourselves up on your most holy faith, praying in the Holy Spirit" (Jude 20). While the New Testament does not specifically teach prayer *through* the Holy Spirit, it does affirm the role of the Holy Spirit as our advocate (John 14:16, 26; 15:26; 16:7).

This brings up a much debated question: "What is praying in the Spirit?" Let us approach the negative first. Praying in the Spirit is the opposite of "vain repetition"—the rather formal repeating of phrases and words that have, over time, become empty of meaning. Praying in the Spirit is not related to a specific location or a specific form of prayer. While these may assist, praying in the Spirit is freedom from repetition, location, or form. Praying in the Spirit is not formal, cold, unemotional praying; it is just the opposite.

Praying in the Spirit means that the Holy Spirit within us directs our praying. It means our prayer is under God's control. This direction and control sometimes leads us to pray for subjects and persons of whom we are not familiar. Wesley Duewel once called praying in the Spirit "God's S.O.S. prayer network."[6]

An illustration of praying in the Spirit happened one Sunday in April 1912. On that night the Titanic struck an iceberg. Colonel Gracy, a passenger on the ship, after helping launch the few life boats that were available, had resigned himself to death. However, as he slipped beneath the waves, his wife at home was suddenly awakened with great concern for her husband. She prayed for several hours, until peace came. Meanwhile Gracy bobbed to the surface near a capsized boat and eventually was rescued. He and his wife later discovered that during the very hours she was agonizing in prayer, he was clinging desperately to this overturned boat.

Still another illustration of praying under the direction of the Holy Spirit is contained in the following story from Argentina:

> Ruth Nolen couldn't get Ed and Linda Ables out of her mind. Ruth and her husband, Steve, are Southern Baptist missionaries in Mendosa, Argentina, 600 miles west of Buenos Aires, where the Ableses are missionaries.
>
> Ruth felt such an impression to pray for the Ableses that she kept trying to call, starting at 10:30 that night, but failing to get through.
>
> Tragically, her fears were well-founded. When Ruth finally reached another missionary in the area, she learned Ed and Linda were in a hospital emergency room being treated for wounds and bruises from a robbery and beatings in their home.
>
> "At the same time that Ruth was praying for us, one of the robbers had cocked a pistol, put it to my head and snapped the trigger," said Ed about the June 15 attack in which he was hit in the head at least a dozen times and in which Linda was struck on the head and in the face.
>
> He figured the gun used by the robbers was empty but police later told him a person could not pull the trigger on such a gun unless it had shells in it. In fact, the gun simply misfired.[7]

Recently much has been written and said about private prayer language. However this is defined and whatever it means to the individual, prayer language is not identical to praying in the Spirit. While praying in the Spirit may for some include their concept of a prayer language, we don't need to have a prayer language to pray in the Spirit.

Praying in the Spirit springs from our awareness of God, of self, of others' needs, and of Christ. Whether or not the prayer is verbal, or an undefined language, "as when the contemplative gazes Godward in love, or the charismatic slips into glossolalia, is immaterial. He [or she] whose heart seeks God through Christ prays in the Spirit."[8]

Having seen prayer *in, with,* and possibly *through* the Holy Spirit, is it proper to pray to the Holy Spirit? There are no examples of this anywhere in scripture, but since the Holy Spirit is God, it may not be wrong to address the Holy Spirit if there is good reason. Prayer to the Spirit may be proper when what we seek from the

Spirit is closer communion with Jesus and Christlikeness in our personal lives.

So, to whom does one pray? R. A. Torrey, the great evangelist, would answer the question with this advice: "To sum it all up, the prayer that God answers is the prayer that is to God the Father, that is on the ground of the atoning blood of God the Son, and that is under the direction and the power of God the Holy Spirit."[9] When you understand that prayer involves all of these, the receiving Father, the providing Son, the directing Spirit, and the praying believer, you realize you are but a channel through whom a current passes. You lose sight of self and determine to pray boldly.

In addition to the Father, the Son, and the Holy Spirit being our heavenly prayer partners, there is also a prayer relationship that involves the angels. They are assigned by God "to render service for the sake of those who will inherit salvation" (Heb. 1:14). There is numerous biblical evidence of the intervention of angels in response to the prayer requests of God's people (see sidebar below).

Are angels still actively involved as partners in prayer today? After my mother underwent major surgery, she confessed to me that prior to it she asked God for assurance—not assurance that she would live through the surgery but assurance that God was still in control. She said someone whom she did not know entered the hospital room. She could not identify the person as a doctor or nurse or any other medical personnel, but such an assurance came that she knew everything was going to be all right. She asked me if this could have been an angel. While there is no proof that the person who entered the room was an angel, neither is there proof that the person wasn't. God may well have sent an angel to respond to my mother's request for assurance.

Scriptures where angels respond to prayer:

Genesis 19

1 Kings 19:5–7

2 Kings 6:17

2 Chronicles 32:20–21

Zechariah 1:8–9

Luke 1:11–13; 23:43

Acts 12:5–10; 27:22–24

Revelation 1:1

Matthew 4:11; 18:10

Further evidence of angelic participation comes in the following account from Ignatius Meimaris, Director of Missions for the Greater Boston Baptist Association:

> I was in graduate school at the time and felt God moving me in the direction of His work. But I wasn't sure. I was trying to verify God's call to the ministry, His desire that I switch from graduate school to seminary.
>
> One day, as I was going from the lab to the church where I worked with youth, I took the subway to downtown Boston. I waited for the train, and, when the doors opened, two older ladies came out. Behind them was a young man wearing a black turtleneck with a black zip-up jacket. As he and I passed, he just patted me on the shoulder very lightly and said, "The Lord is with you brother."
>
> All of a sudden, I felt this tremendous, unexplainable comfort about the ministry and seminary. I naturally turned to see who that person was—maybe somebody I had known. I looked up at the only stairs that were leading from the subway, and there were just the two ladies. He hadn't come out running, so I knew there was no way he would have had the time to run up the forty stairs. It had just been a second and a half. I looked to the left and right to see whether he was standing, waiting for something, but I didn't see one single soul.[10]

In January 1994, Emerging Trends reported that sixty-nine percent of American adults believed in angels and fifty-five percent thought they were spiritual beings created by God with special powers to act as God's agents on earth. With or without the current popularity of angels, this much we know:

- Angels protect God's people (Gen. 32:1; 2 Kings 6:16–17)
- Angels deliver God's people (Acts 12:1–11; Acts 27:23–24)
- Angels deliver God's message to God's people (Luke 2:9–14; Matt. 28:2–7; Acts 10:1–7)
- Angels deliver God's punishment for God's people (Acts 12:23; 2 Chron. 32:20–21)
- Angels renew physical strength (Luke 22:43)

With this knowledge, it is easy to see angels as heavenly partners in prayer.

The realization of the role of angels has been seen in the numerous popular songs and choruses written in recent years. Among them we sing:

> We are standing on holy ground,
> And I know that there are angels all around.
> Let us praise Jesus now.
> We are standing in His presence on holy ground.[11]

The prayer-shaped disciple prays with heavenly prayer partners —*to* the Father; *to* and *in* the name of the Son; *in, with,* and *through* the Holy Spirit; and accompanied by the partnership of angels. But, not only do prayer-shaped disciples have heavenly prayer partners, they also have earthly prayer partners. Let's look at these human partners in prayer.

2. Earthly Prayer Partners:
Where Two or Three Are Gathered

Beyond heavenly prayer partners who receive, respond, and relate, we also have access to human prayer partners. Praying with others is both simple and complex. It is simple in that it's easy to agree to share your prayer needs with one other person or to pray for the needs of another person. It is complex in that it requires time, discipline, concern, and sensitivity. The value of two or more persons praying together is seen in the following paraphrase:

> Two can accomplish more than twice as much as one, ... If one falls, the other pulls him up but if a man falls when he is alone he's in trouble ... and one standing alone can be attacked and defeated, but two can stand back-to-back and conquer; three is even better, for a triple-braided cord is not easily broken (Eccles. 4:9–10, 12, Living Bible).

In the same spirit, Jesus said, "If two of you agree on earth about anything that they may ask, it shall be done for them by My Father who is in heaven. For where two or three have gathered together in

My name, there I am in their midst" (Matt. 18:19–20). While this passage may be related to the judicial and ecclesiastical matters discussed earlier in Matthew 18, the passage may also be related to prayer. The word "asking" means "to pursue a claim." It also means "asking in prayer." Some would limit the term "about anything" to judicial matters, making the promise then that if two individuals in the church come to an agreement concerning any claim that they are pursuing, it will be allowed by the heavenly Father. However, the weight of evidence seems to lean toward the fact that this is a fresh saying, only loosely connected with the passage that precedes it. As the corporate decision of the church is valid in God's sight, so now corporate prayer is powerful with God.

There is a promise made to human prayer partners and that promise is "it shall be done." This is not an isolated idea (see also Matt. 7:7; John 16:23; 1 John 5:15), and yet it is easily misunderstood. Many times two or more persons have agreed on a human level in prayer and received no answer.

We must understand that while there is this promise, there is also a prerequisite required of prayer partners. It is "if two of you agree." The word "agree" is the Greek word *sumphoneo* used for musical instruments that harmonize, but the sounds do not come from identical instruments. Prayer, then, is the very symphony of God, for agreement is reached under the direction of the conductor. Effective prayer is unselfish. It is in agreement with others and with God.

Sometimes we pray over situations and try to include God in our "agreement" when God may not desire to agree or may not even have interest. On one occasion the Baseball Hall of Fame catcher Yogi Berra watched an opposing batter step into the batter's box and make the sign of the cross on home plate. Berra, also a Catholic, simply got up and wiped off the plate with his glove. As he returned to his position he said to the batter, "Why don't we let God just watch this game?" There may be times, for reasons unknown to us, that God decides to "just watch."

When the prerequisite of agreement is met, this promise of answered prayer receives a powerful endorsement described by the phrase "in God's name." You cannot separate God's name from God's purpose or will. You can only pray in God's name if you abide in God (John 15:4–7). This is like a child who can make certain requests of the Father that other children cannot make. You can continue to pray in God's name as you conform to God's image, and you can pray in God's name if you will pray for God's sake. When we are faithful in meeting these human qualifications, the potential of God's power becomes available to prayer partners.

Having seen the promise made, the prerequisite required, and the potential power available to prayer partners, let us take a brief look at what it takes to be a good prayer partner. What should you do when someone asks you to partner with them in prayer? You should begin immediately to pray silently, that is, while they are still describing their request. Not only should you pray for them immediately, but do so by name. This will help you remember the person and the request until you can record it for continued remembrance in prayer. You should also pray for this person consistently. Add their name to your prayer list or into your prayer notebook or diary and pray on a regular or systematic basis. In addition, you should pray for this person specifically. Continue to pray for them by name and pray at the time of their request (such as during the surgery or at a personal encounter or a particular time of testing).

I have practiced this pattern many times when stopped in the church or seminary hallway while on my way to some responsibility. Time did not allow a detailed conversation, much less a time of prayer. By praying immediately, by name, I was able to remember the request and pray more completely at a later time.

The following story illustrates the effectiveness of one person praying for others in a prayer partnership:

> More than half a century ago George Muller, that prince of intercessors with God, began to pray for a group of five personal friends. After five years one of them came to Christ. In ten years two more of them found peace in the same Savior. He prayed on, for twenty-five years, and the fourth man was saved. For the fifth he prayed until the time of his death, and this friend, too, came to

Christ a few months afterward. For this latter friend, Muller had prayed almost fifty-two years! When we behold such perseverance in prayer as this we realize we have scarcely touched the fringe of real importunity in our own intercessions for others.[1]

Many times the family provides a resource of prayer partners. When Jesus Christ becomes Lord of the family, a new authority is in place and a new attitude invades the family, and there is a new affirmation of individual and family worth. If the family is to grow in their relationship to Jesus Christ, it is only natural that a part of that growth would be family prayer. The strength of the family may well be determined by how well family members support each other as prayer partners. Sad indeed are the words of one minister, "In some forty years of ministering to those who have come to me for help with marriage problems, I have never found a couple who recalled having received any instruction in prayer as part of their premarital preparation."[2]

The family, serving as prayer partners, offers great opportunities to pray for and with the children, thus teaching them how to pray. In praying for your children, the following scriptural guide may be helpful:

1. Pray for their salvation (2 Tim. 3:15).
2. Pray they will hate sin (Ps. 97:10).
3. Pray they will select the right kind of friends (Prov. 1:10).
4. Pray the Holy Spirit will be poured out on them (Isa. 44:3–5).
5. Pray they will be identified as children blessed by the Lord (Isa. 61:9).
6. Pray God will protect them from making the wrong choices (Hos. 2:6).
7. Pray they will be protected from Satan (John 17:15).
8. Pray they will present themselves to God (Rom. 12:1).
9. Pray they will not conform to the world (Rom. 12:2).
10. Pray they will respect authority (Rom. 13:1).
11. Pray they will respect their body as a temple of the Holy Spirit (1 Cor. 6:18–19).

12. Pray that, if they marry, they will marry another believer (2 Cor. 6:14–17).

13. Pray they will be submissive to God in all things (James 4:7).

14. Pray they will tell their children of the things of God (Ps. 78:4).

On the other hand, praying together as a family allows you to teach the children to pray. Here are some suggestions in helping children learn how to pray:

1. *Set an example.* When you pray with a small child, pray simply so that he or she can pray as you do. Use short sentences and simple words such as "Thank you for Jesus," "Bless my teacher," and "Help Grandma get well."

2. *Never criticize your children's prayers.* They are not praying to you, but to God—their loving, heavenly Father. Allow your children to express themselves freely to God. If they are criticized, they may regard prayer from a negative perspective. As they grow older they might abandon prayer, feeling that either you or God will not find their prayers acceptable.

3. *Never insist that your children pray aloud.* You may find an exception to this rule, but it would indeed be rare. Children, and especially teenagers, may go through periods when they are hesitant about praying in front of others. Offer them the opportunity, but don't insist.

4. *Use conversational prayer.* Let each member of the family pray a sentence, then stop and allow someone else to pray. Parents can lead children from one area to another by introducing new topics and allowing the children to follow with items of their own.

5. *Vary body positions as you pray.* Variety helps children understand that no matter where they are, they can pray.

6. *Use lists and pictures.* Maintain a family prayer list. In a notebook, write down items to be thankful for and requests for the family and other people. When you hear of a response or answer from God, jot that in the notebook next to the

request. Your children will see firm evidence that God answers prayer. Keep a photo album of people for whom you pray. Younger children need a point of reference for their prayers.

7. *Teach your children to pray BIG to increase their faith.* When they pray for things that seem impossible from their point of view and find that God answers, their faith is given a tremendous boost.[3]

8. *Teach your children to trust God.* When the prayer requests of your children are not answered according to their desires, you are afforded an excellent opportunity to teach them how to pray in faith and accept God's response, even when it is different from our own. While difficult even for mature believers, if this lesson can be imparted to a child, it might prevent a faltering faith in adulthood.

What if one or more members of the family is an unwilling partner in prayer? Then those whose desire it is to pray, must pray alone for all members of the family, hoping for the day when the entire family can pray together. The one who prays becomes God's door into the family. The privilege of being God's door is matched by responsibility. You are most responsible for the one to whom you are most closely related.

Another form of prayer partners is the small group. The small prayer group is defined as: "A prayer cell is any small group united in the Spirit of Christ to pray and to seek together the highest in God's purpose."[4] As to the unique nature of the small prayer group, author William Sangster comments, "Something seems to be added to prayers offered in fellowship which is not available in the same measure to the same prayers offered by the same people in separation."[5] Dietrich Bonhoeffer writes:

> ... the first condition that makes it possible for an individual to pray for the group is the intercession of all the others for him and for his prayers. How can one person pray the prayer of the fellowship without being steadied and upheld in prayer by the fellowship itself? At

this very point, every word of criticism must be transformed into fervent intercession and brotherly help. Otherwise how easily might a fellowship be broken asunder right here![6]

For the most part, small prayer groups are involved in intercessory prayer for others. The first kind of intercessory prayer within small groups is the prayer *using the name of another group member.* "Lord, thank you for demonstrating your love for Heather this week." In essence, love is given and shared within the group. No request is necessary from a group member for a prayer of love to be offered. The second type is a prayer of *blessing.* This can be a one-sentence prayer, simply asking God to bless someone. As to the content of the blessing, it should be made as specific as possible. A third kind is the prayer of *asking.* Two or more persons agree on a specific request, and they ask God to respond to that request. The fourth kind is the prayer of *receiving.* This is simply a prayer giving thanks to God in anticipation of response to the prayers offered.

In beginning a small prayer group the key word is "concern." If you are concerned about things such as spiritual renewal, spiritual growth, or spiritual warfare, you are probably concerned enough to begin a small prayer group. The first step in beginning one is to rededicate your own life to Christ and to the ministry of intercessory prayer. The person who originates the group will need all the spiritual resources available. Thus, a rededication not only calls forth those resources but allows the creator of the prayer group to begin with a fresh start.

Next you should seek God's leadership as to who should be invited to participate and when and where the group should meet. The makeup of the group may consist of family members, business associates meeting at noon, employees on a coffee break, friends forming a breakfast club, married couples, single adults, students meeting before classes early in the morning, mothers meeting when they drop off their kindergartners, or many other variations.

As you talk to various friends and associates about the idea of a prayer group, listen for those who share the same concern. As those who are interested are found, begin seeking God's will as to a time and a place and then begin inviting those interested persons to participate in the group.

Special attention must be given to the agenda for a small prayer group meeting. At all costs avoid a "rushed" feeling. A proper time and place will help you avoid this. The place and time should lend itself to a casual, leisurely approach to prayer. Allow time for getting acquainted with the other group members on a spiritual level. Needs and prayer requests should always be shared during the meeting as well as victories and items of praise.

Prior to the first meeting you will have to determine if the group is going to remain the same size or if it is to be enlarged as time goes by. If the group is to grow, a maximum should be set to limit the number of participants. Experience has shown that when a group exceeds ten or twelve, it becomes too large for its original purpose. Thus, if the group is allowed to grow, plans should be made to divide the group every time it reaches ten or twelve persons.

Next, find a leader. The person who had the original idea for the prayer group may not necessarily be the best person to lead it. Besides having a deep desire to pray for and pray with others, the leader must be a motivator. The leader must have some organizational ability as well as the ability to facilitate discussion in the group. The group leader will also be required to make meeting arrangements and periodic adjustments.

Several years ago, I attended a seminar at the Trinity Evangelical Divinity School in Deerfield, Illinois, led by Robert E. Coleman. During the course of the seminar, Dr. Coleman shared with us stories about his group of seminary students with whom he met for prayer early on Wednesday mornings before classes began. He said that much of what he had written in the last few years had come from ideas which were born in this small group. I had been thinking about doing something similar in my teaching responsibilities at Southwestern Baptist Theological Seminary in Fort Worth, Texas. This gave me the last bit of motivation necessary. As the fall semester approached, I asked God to impress upon my mind the names of six or eight young men whom I should invite. I determined that we would meet on Wednesdays in my office from 12:00 to 1:00 P.M., and that we would bring a sack lunch. As we ate, we would share prayer concerns and praises. This allowed us approximately twenty-five to thirty minutes for actual prayer. As God impressed names on my mind, I wrote a letter to each student asking if he would consider participation for one semester. Once the group was intact, we met that first Wednesday of the fall semester.

Every semester following, the make-up of the prayer group has been a bit different as class schedules and other responsibilities prevent some from continuing in the group. Each time there is an opening I ask God to impress upon me the names of new students who ought to be a part of this group. From time to time, we have expanded the group to include four or five couples meeting in our home and praying with my wife and me on Thursday evenings from 6:00 to 7:00 P.M. Occasionally, the group has met early on Thursday mornings before the beginning of classes. The response of the students has not only been positive, but I find I anticipate this hour more than any other hour of the week. It has proven to be one of the highlights of my teaching experience.

As the years have gone by, I have kept in correspondence with many former members of this intercessory prayer group. In fact, these men are among those mentioned in the Acknowledgments section of this book. It is rewarding to know the impact made on their lives through this group and to see them developing intercessory prayer groups in their own various ministries.

Should you decide to create a small prayer group, there are some practical suggestions that ought to be heeded. In the first place, proper preparation of minds and hearts is always necessary at the beginning of each prayer session. Time for meditation and silent reflection ought to be offered. There is always a tendency during the prayer time to panic if silence goes for too long. This silence should not cause undue concern but should be a time for reflection and contemplation. In a small prayer group, the leader and perhaps even the members should strive to always pray outside the group. That is, never let the group's focus turn totally inward to the point that members are only praying for each other. Work at including prayer requests from outside the group even to the point of praying for some items which have no direct relationship to any group member.

As the group continues to pray, your list of ongoing prayer requests may become so long that the leader will need to prioritize the items. One alternative to all members praying for every request is to divide the list and have group members pray in teams of two rather than in the circle of eight-to-ten. The group member should lead in praying expectantly, anticipating clear answers to the prayer requests. Persistence is another trait which should characterize small prayer groups. Do not be afraid of praying for the same concerns meeting after meeting. By all means the small prayer group should be related somehow to a local church or churches. Never should a small prayer group become a substitute for the local church in the life of an individual. It should supplement and complement the ministry of the local church.

One final practical suggestion is to allow the natural to happen without changing the purpose of the prayer group. Prayer naturally leads to ministry and service. Much of the church's efforts in the past to reach needy individuals has assumed that one person—usually the minister—could bear responsibility for helping maybe ten people, if not hundreds. We have now learned that real ministry calls for a reversal of this ratio. It may well take ten committed, praying persons to serve as the means through which God brings about change in the life of a single man or woman. If the small prayer group continues to pray for a specific concern, its members will naturally develop a burden for the person related to that concern and want to reach out in ministry and service. While the prayer group should allow this to happen, it should guard against allowing the group to become a ministry/service group rather than a prayer group unless the group decides to totally change its purpose for existing.

One semester, my seminary group included a student who had just married. A few weeks after the wedding, his wife discovered a large mole that was eventually diagnosed as a rare form of malignant melanoma. Because the student needed to be with his wife in the hospital, the group met in her hospital room for our weekly prayer time. While we prayed during the hour, we also became a ministry group. Upon her arrival home from the hospital, we helped supply them with enough food so she would not have to cook until she regained her strength. Even with this needed ministry, we were quick to return to our original purpose of being a prayer group that ministered rather than allowing ourselves to become a ministry group that prayed.

While many small groups function effectively, there are no doubt many others that cease to exist shortly after their beginning. Thus, it is good to look at what causes a prayer group to die. One reason they die is a failure to keep prayer as the clear purpose of the group. Sometimes ministry or service takes the place of prayer in the group. More often, the one-hour meeting time becomes more and more occupied with fellowship and social interaction and less and less devoted to prayer. A prayer group that begins with too many members may die for the lack of personal attention to each one's requests and praises. Often prayer groups become ingrown; that is, they pray only for their own needs rather than reaching beyond their needs to the needs of the community and indeed the needs of the world.

In addition to the above reasons, prayer groups sometimes die because personal prayer requests become items of gossip. This breaks down the trust level of the group and results in group members refusing to share personal requests.

Recently, I was having some pain in my left shoulder and shared this as an item of prayer with some of those who are close to me. I had already made a doctor's appointment, but I wanted prayer support as I sought the reason for my pain. One person shared with another that I was not only having pain in my shoulder, but they were afraid it was related to my heart. The person with whom the "heart" addition had been shared proceeded to share in a public prayer meeting at his church that "prayer was needed for Professor Crawford of our seminary who is having heart problems." There were seminary students present in that prayer meeting who proceeded to form a prayer chain to pray on my behalf. Unfortunately, Christmas vacation came at that precise time. The first day back, I found when I entered my secretary's office a student who turned and looked at me with a shocked expression and asked, "Are you all right?" When I responded that I was indeed feeling fine, he said, "We've all been praying for you." I asked why. He said, "You had a heart attack right before Christmas!" One person's prayer concern became another person's item of gossip. In reality, the pain in the left shoulder was caused by a calcium spur between the sixth and seventh vertebrae of my back and had no direct relationship whatsoever to my heart.

Some prayer groups cease to exist because the emphasis of the group becomes negative instead of positive. Few people want to attend a one-hour prayer time where everyone is grieving over sad conditions of life around them. The leader of the group must always work to find a balance between the negative and the positive.

Finally, prayer groups may die because one member dominates the discussion time. If one person always has a "better" or "more dramatic" prayer request than everybody else, it will soon grow old. Likewise, if one person knows everything about every request and feels obligated to share all they know, the prayer group will soon cease to exist.

Small prayer groups are confronted with potential problems. However, if the leader is committed to moving the group along in the proper manner, and the group is aware of Christ's presence (Matt. 18:19–20) and willing to share each other's burdens (Gal. 6:2), the small prayer group can be a powerful force for intercession in God's kingdom.

A former member of my prayer group, having graduated several semesters ago, sent a request to the present group. Even though he knew no one in the group, he knew we would be faithful to intercede for him at a specific time. The request shared a major decision that the former student needed to make and requested that we join him in prayer as he prayed alone at the very time of our scheduled weekly meeting. Later another he called thanked the group, and informed us of discernment that had come to him even as we prayed together across the miles.

So even as Jesus responds as our enthroned heavenly prayer partner, and the Holy Spirit responds as our indwelling heavenly prayer partner, and angels respond as our accompanying heavenly prayer partners, so friends and family make up our supportive human prayer partners. What more could we ask when it comes to prayer partnerships?

We have seen the prayer-shaped disciple's earthly prayer partners—friends, family, and small-group members. Now with both heavenly and earthly prayer partners established, it is altogether appropriate to wonder what kind of responses we may expect from God as we pray and as we are joined in prayer.

3. Awareness of God's Responses:
Listen Up

God always responds to prayer. God might not grant our every wish and desire, but the sincere prayers of believers are always answered. Indeed there is a vast difference between petitions that are not granted and what we sometimes call unanswered prayer. While we may not get everything for which we ask, we always receive an answer from God. Our problem in understanding this is we pray to God with a full confidence that God has the power to answer our prayers. Yet we do not afford God the authority to answer our requests in God's own fashion. Therefore we falsely say, "God did not answer." Let us look, then, at some of the answers we might expect God to give to our prayers.

Sometimes God's answer to our prayer is "no." This was the answer given by Jesus to two would-be followers when they requested to first "bury my father" and "say good-bye to those at home" (Luke 9:57–62). He also said no to a mother who requested that her two sons might sit on his right hand and left hand in the kingdom (Matt. 20:20–23). God told Jesus no in response to the prayer at

Gethsemane to "let this cup pass" (Matt. 26:36-48; Mark 14:32-42; Luke 22:39-46). We must not get discouraged when God gives us a "no" answer. For indeed, only children demand a happy ending to every story. How old do we have to be before we realize even prayer can't get us everything we selfishly desire? An unknown poet wrote:

> I asked of God that He should give success
> To the high task I sought for Him to do;
> I asked that every hindrance might grow less
> And that my hours of weakness might be few;
> I asked that far and lofty heights be scaled—
> And now I humbly thank Him that I failed
>
> For with the pain and sorrow came to me
> A dower of tenderness in act and thought;
> And with the failure came a sympathy,
> An insight which success had never brought.
> Father, I had been foolish and unblest
> If Thou hadst granted me my blind request.

What can you do when God gives you a "no" response? Rejoice that God heard your prayer and responded. Pray again and ask God to teach you in the midst of the "no." Evaluate your prayer to see if it was in keeping with God's will and if not, why wasn't it? Allow God to work in your life through the "no."

We must learn, as did the Apostle Paul, that when we are told "no," God has another solution to our request. Paul said about his thorn in the flesh, "Concerning this I implored the Lord three times that it might leave me. And He has said to me, 'My grace is sufficient for you'" (2 Cor. 12:8-9). Sometimes a "no" answer is a way of letting us know that God's grace is sufficient for our every need.

I finished leading a conference in Pensacola, Florida, and looked everywhere for the person who was to take me to the airport for the flight to my next speaking engagement in New Orleans. When he finally arrived I realized that the chances of my catching this flight were growing slim. As my driver rushed furiously through the traffic, I asked God to help me catch the flight so I would not be late for my next assignment. I missed the flight by just a few minutes. As I waited for the next flight, I was having my own private pity party in a corner of the airport lounge. After all, wasn't I doing God's work? So why would God allow me to waste time sitting in this airport? Then came an announcement for those awaiting my re-scheduled flight. We reported as instructed to the proper airline gate only to be told that our airplane, which normally made round trips from Pensacola to New Orleans, would not be keeping its schedule. It had crashed on landing at New Orleans. Had I made my initial flight on time, I would have been on the plane that crashed. I thanked God for a "no" answer.

Sometimes God's answer is "yes." The experience of the disciples in the upper room after the ascension of Jesus might be interpreted as a yes: "When they had prayed, the place where they had gathered together was shaken" (Acts 4:31). James shares a more obvious illustration: Elijah "prayed earnestly that it would not rain, and it did not rain on the earth for three years and six months. Then he prayed again, and the sky poured rain" (James 5:17-18). A still more obvious yes is in the life of Jabez who prayed that God would enlarge the borders: "And God granted him what he requested" (1 Chron. 4:10). When Moses asked to see God's glory it was granted (Exod. 33:18-23). When Moses interceded on behalf of the people who had been bitten by serpents and were dying, God responded with a yes and the people lived (Num. 21:6-9). Surely this is the kind of answer the psalmist had in mind when he wrote of God, "You have given him his heart's desire, and You have not withheld the request of his lips" (Ps. 21:2).

An Associated Press article showed a yes answer for Cindy Hartman's prayer when she encountered a pistol-toting burglar in her home. Hartman, of Conway, Arkansas, said the burglar confronted her when she came in to answer the phone. He ripped the cord out of the wall and ordered her into a cramped bedroom closet. Then she dropped to her knees.

"I asked if I could pray for him," she said.

Hartman said the man apologized, used a shirt to wipe his fingerprints from the gun, and he even dropped to his knees to join

Hartman in prayer. Then he yelled to a woman in a pickup truck, "We've got to unload all of this and return it. This is a Christian family. We can't do this to them."

Elizabeth Barrett Browning wrote in her poem "Aurora Leigh, II, 6":

> God answers sharp and sudden on some prayers,
> And thrusts the thing we have prayed for in our face,
> A gauntlet with a gift in it.

Then there are times when God's answer is "wait." When asked to wait, we often feel as though our prayers are unanswered. In reality, we have received a conditional answer. When a woman of Canaan requested of Jesus that he heal her daughter, the answer she received was "wait" (Matt. 15:22-28). When the disciples were ready to spread the good news of the resurrection of Christ, God's response to them was, "You are to stay in the city until you are clothed with power from on high" (Luke 24:49). Mark 11:25-26 and Matthew 6:12 indicate our request for forgiveness always receives a "wait" from God, dependent upon our willingness to forgive those who have wronged us. Immediately after his conversion, Paul prayed for a mission, an assignment (Acts 9:6). God sent him into the solitude of Arabia to wait. A "wait" answer sometimes tries our patience but always challenges our persistence. Indeed, we are not "praying to an incomprehensible abstraction whose providence is limited by our comprehension. We are praying to a gracious, loving, sympathizing, condescending God who delights in our troublesome persistence."[1]

Kathryn Blackburn Peck wrote:

> In the moment of its crying
>   Came no answer to my heart,
> But, long-deferred, it came with blessing
>   In a quiet place apart.
> Seldom in the midst of toiling
>   Do we reap our recompense.
> It may come when hands are folded
>   In a sunset hour long hence.
> Not in thunderous crash of earth-quake,
>   Not in whirlwind or in fire,

Not in voice of sounding trumpet
    Does God speak our deep desire.
But with strife and fretting over—
    Waiting—all serene and still,
We may hear the whispered message
    Teaching us His perfect will.
When we school our hearts to patience
    God reveals His better way.
Providing oft that His tomorrow
    is far better than today.

Once, in the city of Antwerp, a traveler watched Belgian peasants weaving a tapestry. Though he searched carefully, he saw nothing but a dark and meaningless mass. There was not a single clue as to what was being fashioned. Seeing that he was perplexed, one of the weavers stopped work and led him to the other side. There he stood spellbound as he looked upon a beautiful design coming to completion, thread by thread, strand by strand. We grow impatient waiting on an answer to our requests, but if we persist perhaps we will be allowed to see the answer from God's perspective. When a "wait" answer comes, understand that God wants us to persist even during our waiting.

In the words of Mrs. F. G. Burroughs in "Sometime, Somewhere":

Unanswered yet, the prayers your lips have pleaded
In agony of heart these many years?
Does faith begin to fail, is hope declining,
And think you all in vain those falling tears?
Say not the Father has not heard your prayer,
You shall have your desire, sometime, somewhere!

Unanswered yet? Tho' when you first presented
This one petition at the Father's throne,
It seemed you could not wait the time of asking,
So anxious was your heart to have it done:
If years have passed since then, do not despair,
For God will answer you sometime, somewhere.

Unanswered yet? But you are not unheeded;
The promises of God forever stand;

To Him our days and years alike are equal.
"Have faith in God!" It is your Lord's command.
Hold on to Jacob's angel, and your prayer
Shall bring a blessing down sometime, somewhere.

Unanswered yet? Nay, do not say unanswered;
Perhaps your part is not yet wholly done.
The work began when first your prayer was uttered,
And God will finish what He has begun.
Keep incense burning at the shrine of prayer,
And glory shall descend, sometime, somewhere.

Unanswered yet? Faith cannot be unanswered;
Her feet are firmly planted on the Rock.
Amid the wildest storms she stands undaunted,
Nor quails before the loudest thunder shock.
She knows Omnipotence has heard her prayer,
And cries, "It shall be done, sometime, somewhere."

Furthermore, I think God's answer is occasionally "we'll see." Prayer is often illustrated in the terminology of earthly children requesting of their earthly father. My children would say my favorite answer is "we'll see." However, just like many earthly fathers know what is best for their children on most occasions, so the heavenly Father knows what is best for his children on all occasions. Sometimes the best response to a request is "we'll see."

Several Christmases ago we had hardly finished opening the packages when my children, surrounded by wrapping paper, requested, "Can we spend next Christmas with Uncle Bob in Nashville?" My response was "we'll see." Not only was their timing poor, but the proper answer was too far in the future to share with them. In reality, by the next Christmas Uncle Bob had married Aunt Linda and moved to the Memphis area. Had I answered their question "yes," I would have been unable to keep my word. Had I answered "no," I would have been untruthful, since we did spend a portion of next Christmas with Uncle Bob in Memphis with Aunt Linda. The "wait" might have sufficed but a "we'll see" answer seemed to be appropriate.

This "we'll see" answer does not detract from the sovereignty of God. God waits for a "fullness of time" to respond to the requests of his children. Prayers related to material benefits, removal of difficulties, and healing are sometimes answered "we'll see." Prayer from a human perspective is what makes it possible for God to change his mind without being in the least inconsistent. The next time you feel God has answered you with a we'll see, allow him the privilege of being sovereign and having a change of mind without being inconsistent.

Occasionally, God's answer to our prayer is "what about this?" This answer comes especially when God's answer is different from our request. In Psalm 106:15, God "gave them their request, but sent a wasting disease among them." They obviously got more than they requested. Further biblical precedent for this is seen in Deuteronomy 3:23-27, John 11, and 2 Corinthians 12:8-9. On other occasions, "what about this?" comes to us when God's answer exceeds our request, such as in 1 Kings 3:7-14; 19:3-8; and 2 Chronicles 1:10-12. In Acts 12:5-15 God responded with Peter's release from prison when, in all probability, the believers were only praying for his safety.

Sometimes God's answer is "what about this?" when a better way is known, as illustrated by Jesus in the parable of the prodigal son. The son went home to ask of the father that he be received as a hired servant. The answer was a much better plan. He was restored as a son (Luke 15:17-24). Likewise, the disciples seemed to be amazed at the response of Jesus to still the storm when they had simply informed him that they were perishing. I'm not sure what request the disciples had in mind, but they obviously got more than they imagined (Luke 8:24-25).

Monica, the mother of Augustine, prayed for years for the salvation of her sinful son. On one occasion, Monica prayed all night that Augustine would not set sail for Rome as he had planned and where he would surely sink further into sin. Actually Augustine left for Rome as Monica was praying. Contrary to Monica's specific request, God said "what about this?" and led Augustine on the journey to meet Ambrose, who led Augustine to Christ.

The idea that God cannot negotiate an answer with spiritual children is false. Often in scripture and in personal experience, a prayer request is a negotiable request and God responds with "what about this?" Consider King Manasseh, who butchered prophets and saints alike and led God's people to "do more evil than the nations whom the Lord destroyed before the sons of Israel" (2 Chron. 33:9). God had promised to destroy Manasseh and "abandon the remnant of My inheritance and deliver them into the hand of their enemies" (2 Kings 21:14). However, as a miserable old man, captive in a foreign prison, Manasseh "entreated the Lord his God and humbled himself greatly before the God of his fathers" (2 Chron. 33:12). God responded, not with promised destruction, but with a "what about this?"—a blessing on the people.

Another example was when God had promised through Jonah, "Forty days and Nineveh will be overthrown" (Jon. 3:4). The great city of Nineveh, from its king to its populace, humbled themselves in prayer and fasting, repented before God, and cried out for forgiveness. Hearing their prayers, "God relented concerning the calamity which He had declared He would bring upon them. And He did not do it" (Jon. 3:10).

Don't forget the prayer of King Hezekiah. God said to him, "Set your house in order, for you shall die and not live" (2 Kings 20:1). However, following the pleas of Hezekiah, God said, "I will add fifteen years to your life" (2 Kings 20:6).

We have been reminded by Charles Finney that "the objection to prayer, that God is unchangeable, and therefore cannot turn aside to hear prayer, is altogether a fallacy and the result of ignorance."[2] Therefore, allow God the privilege of answering you with a "what about this?" that might lead to further communication and even negotiation regarding God's response to your prayer. Remember that God is "able to do far more abundantly beyond all that we ask or think" (Eph. 3:20).

The following poem illustrates in a beautiful way how God sometimes gives us that which is different from our requests:

He asked for strength that he might achieve;
    he was made weak that he might obey.
He asked for health that he might do greater things;
    he was given infirmity that he might do better things.
He asked for riches that he might be happy;
    he was given poverty that he might be wise.
He asked for power that he might have the praise of men;
    he was given weakness that he might feel the need of God.
He asked for all things that he might enjoy life;
    he was given life that he might enjoy all things.
He has received nothing that he has asked for, all that he hoped for,
    his prayer is answered.[3]

From a lighter perspective, there is one further response that God occasionally is tempted to give to prayers. That response is "you've got to be joking!" This answer sometimes comes to Christians when their faith is too small. Seldom, if ever, did Jesus rebuke his disciples for expecting too much from him. Often they were rebuked for expecting too little from him. Sometimes our faith is so small that when we make a request of God, he is amused. He would have given us much more if we had only asked. One of the great surprises of the Christian life is what God finally gives us is far better than what we originally asked.

On other occasions God may answer "you've got to be joking!" when our self-confidence is too large. There are occasions in the lives of Christians when we request of God only that which we know we can produce if God doesn't. We often do this in church related activities as we set goals that are within reach, rather than setting goals that we could reach only with God's help. In other words, we attempt to guarantee our answers, and God must be amused by this endeavor. Allow God the privilege to respond with "you've got to be joking!" Laugh at yourself when this happens, learn from the experience, and continue in prayer.

But what about the silence of God? Children are often frustrated when their requests are met with silence from a parent. We are no different. Only through time spent with God and maturity of faith, will you learn how to interpret God's silence. It may mean "wait" or "we'll see" or "no," but the silence never means absence. God is near you even in the silence. Listen more intently. Walk more closely. There is always a response, even in the silence, even when we don't know it.

Now that we've discussed some of God's responses, let's consider some of the basic ingredients of prayer. The prayer-shaped disciple begins with the basics.

4. Basic Ingredients:
ACTing Up

For many years, believers have prayed through the traditional acronym ACTS as a means of covering four basic ingredients of prayer. Later we will explore ingredients beyond these four, but for now, let's look at these.

The *A* denotes Adoration, or Praise, as demonstrated in Psalm 150. This includes praising God for who he is. It centers on the nature and character of God. The words of George Buttrick say it all:

> He consented to a messy little gallows set up on the city dump. He asked nothing for Himself, except to love God and men. He courted oblivion. He should have been lost in the ruck of history. But He keeps coming back: lovers and liars, Kings and Commoners, the Mafia and the misfit saints, all date their letters from His birthday. The centuries have knelt before Him daringly. The cross is empty now, yet never empty. It has stolen the skyline of every city. All prayer begins in that adoration.[1]

To praise God is to bless him, attributing honor and glory to the Lord. It is to speak of God's wonders while standing in awe of who God is. George W. Frazer wrote:

> God our Father, We adore Thee!
> We, thy children, bless thy name!
> Chosen in the Christ before thee.
> We are "without blame."
> We adore thee! We adore thee!
> Abba's praises we proclaim!
> We adore thee! We adore thee!
> Abba's praises we proclaim!

The Bible is filled with experiences of praise (see sidebar).

The Old Testament words for praise involved sound and related mostly to public worship. Some have felt this should continue to be true exclusively. However, many others have felt that praise has silent, private applications as well. Horatius Bonar, the hymn writer, wrote:

> Fill Thou my life, O Lord my God,
>   In every part with praise,
> That my whole being may proclaim
>   Thy being and Thy ways.
>
> Not for the lip of praise alone,
>   Nor e'en the praising heart,
> I ask, but for a life made up
>   of praise in every part.

So, whether we praise in public or private, we must see adoration as a vital ingredient of prayer. It always has been. In fact, many of us grew up singing this chorus:

> Praise Him! Praise Him!
> All ye little children
> God is love! God is love!

What happened to praise? It seems as though its priority got misplaced through the years. We developed a falsehood in the church that our first priority is other people. Our first priority is to God, offering praise and desiring to please. Furthermore, praise is an act of verbalized worship or adoration declaring or acknowledging God for who he is, while thanksgiving is an act of offering specific thanks to God for things he has done, is doing, and will do.

Praise God for who he is—Wonderful Counselor, Mighty God, Everlasting Father, Prince of Peace. Originally addressed to people facing perplexity and impending danger, the words of Hebrews speak to us: "Through Him then, let us continually offer up a sacrifice of praise to God" (Heb. 13:15).

Paul E. Billheimer's oft-quoted work helps us understand the importance of praise:

> Here is one of the greatest values of praise: It decentralizes self. The worship and praise of God demands a shift of center from self to God. One cannot praise God without relinquishing occupation with self. Praise produces forgetfulness of self—and forgetfulness of self is health.[2]

Praise possesses several dimensions. It obviously focuses our attention on God. While we are giving thanks, our thoughts still center on self, but when we praise, our souls ascend to selfless adoration and focus only on the majesty and power of God. Praise cleanses our lives by shutting the door on intruding ideas originating from self or Satan. Praise increases faith. The more you praise, the more you trust. Praise limits Satan. Hezekiah and Isaiah defeated their enemies by praise. Since our enemy is Satan, we can do likewise.

Biblical examples of when God is praised:

The children of Israel praised God for being the deliverer at the Red Sea (Exod. 15).
Hannah praised God for giving her Samuel (1 Sam. 2:1–10).
David praised God for being good (Pss. 100, 103, 106, 107).
Ezra praised God for being the deliverer from Babylon (Ezra 7:27).
Paul praised God for being wise (Rom. 11:33–36).
The hosts of heaven praised God for being the Redeemer (Rev. 5:8–14; 7:9–12).

Psalm 113 gives several aspects of praise. It defines the object of praise: "Praise the LORD"; "Praise the name of the LORD" (v. 1). The object of praise is the Lord or the name of the Lord or some description of the Lord: "my strength," "my redeemer," the "rock of our salvation" (Ps. 95:1). Further, this psalm identifies the participants in praise: "O servants of the Lord" (v. 1). It may be "I" or "my soul" (Ps. 103:1; 104:1) or "Your Godly ones" (Ps. 145:10) or "the congregation" (Ps. 149:2) or "the redeemed of the Lord" (Ps. 107:2) or "everything that has breath" (Ps. 150:6), or all the works of nature (Ps. 89:5, 96:11, 97:1, 98:4). Psalm 113 sets forth the duration of praise: "from the rising of the sun to its setting" (v. 3). Praise is continuous: regular days and holidays, morning and night, good days and bad days. In addition, you can praise God from any location (see sidebar). The psalm states the reason for praise: "The Lord is high above all nations; His glory is above the heavens" (vs. 4–5). Because the Lord is exalted above all, we must offer praise.

What are the means through which we express our praise?

- Praise is to be sung: "Sing for joy in the Lord, O you righteous ones; Praise is becoming to the upright" (Ps. 33:1).
- Praise is to be expressed in public: "I will praise You among a mighty throng" (Ps. 35:18).
- Praise is to be proclaimed: "That I may tell of all Your praises" (Ps. 9:14).
- Praise is to be shouted for joy: "My lips will shout for joy when I sing praises to You" (Ps. 71:23).
- Praise is to be expressed with music: "It is good to praise the Lord and make music to your name, O Most High" (Ps. 92:1 NIV).
- Praise is to be spoken: "I will bless the Lord at all times; His praise shall continually be in my mouth" (Ps. 34:1).

Psalm 103 lists for us numerous benefits of praise. "Praise the Lord, O my soul; all my inmost being, praise his holy name. Praise the Lord, O my soul, and forget not all his benefits" (Ps. 103:1-2 NIV). Take a look at the "benefits" which begin in verse 3. I count eighteen, and this is only a sample of the benefits of praising God.

Finally the Bible offers us a word of praise: "Hallelujah!" We ought to praise God for who God is now, but also to get ready for heaven. "Hallelujah" comes from two Hebrew words which mean "Praise" and "Jehovah." We say, "Praise the Lord!" "Hallelujah" is a word that is reportedly

Examples of praising God in trying times:
Jonah was in a large fish when he praised God (Jon. 2:1–8).
Daniel was constantly on the edge of disaster yet praised God (Dan. 9:4–6).
Jeremiah was seen as a loser in life and a weeping prophet, yet he praised God (Jer. 32:17–22).
David, while praying for mercy and forgiveness, shifted to praise (Ps. 86:1–8).

the same in every language. The God who confused the languages in Genesis 11 apparently left one word the same in all languages—Hallelujah. Get used to it; you will hear it often in heaven (Rev. 19:1-6). "Praise honors God, brings joy to the angels, and strikes terror in any evil spirit which may be around. Praise clears the atmosphere, washes your spirit, multiplies your faith, and clothes you with God's presence and power."[3] The hymn writer Timothy Dudley-Smith helps us with his words:

> Praise the Lord and bless his Name,
> life and peace in him are found.
> All his benefits proclaim,
> grace with love and mercy crowned:
>> Sins forgiven, strength restored!
>> Sing, my soul, and praise the Lord!
>
> High as heaven's furthest star,
> vaster than the shores of space,
> so he bears our sins afar,
> so he brings to us his grace.
>> He who hears his children's prayer
>> ever keeps us in his care.
>
> Swifter than the winds that pass,
> fading as the summer flowers,

what though all our days are grass?
faith and hope shall still be ours.
    God's unchanging love is sure
    and endures for evermore.

Praise the Lord of earth and heaven,
angel hosts about his throne,
sinners by his grace forgiven,
saints who his dominion own:
    God of all, by all adored!
    Sing, my soul, and praise the Lord![4]

The next letter, *C*, denotes Confession as demonstrated in many passages. Confession is a perennial need and allows us to receive God's forgiveness. It is an admission of sin and the need for repentance and forgiveness. When we confess our sins, God forgives them, reassures us of unconditional love, and encourages us to holy living. One problem which prevents confession is a reluctance to admit to our misdeeds. A casual attitude toward sin makes confession seem unnecessary. Confession comes hard for those who are unwilling to expose their very souls, even to God.

Confession before God is imperative for the believer who desires to remain in harmonious fellowship with God. The biblical evidence for this is ample (see sidebar). Not only is confession a must, but scripture commands specific confession. Levitical law says, "So it shall be when he becomes guilty in one of these, that he shall confess that in which he has sinned" (Lev. 5:5). To sin is a generic term covering a variety of wrong actions. To confess is to identify specific actions and seek forgiveness for them.

Confession scriptures:

Psalm 66:18–19
Isaiah 59:2
Jeremiah 5:25
Daniel 9:20
Matthew 6:12
Luke 5:8; 11:4
Hebrews 12:1–2
James 5:16
1 John 1:8–10

There are those who argue that since Jesus died for all sin on the cross, we need not ask for further forgiveness. They often quote the verse that says Jesus has "forgiven us all our transgressions, having canceled out the certificate of debt . . . having nailed it to the cross" (Col. 2:13-14). Granted, Jesus died for all sin and in so doing allowed for the forgiveness of all future sin. However, God desires that we continue to both acknowledge our wrongs and ask for forgiveness for known sin.

Just like the loving parent encourages the disobedient child to "say you're sorry," so the loving Father desires us to admit guilt, not just acknowledge it. I can acknowledge my wrong without seeking forgiveness or repenting of sin. Acknowledgement simply means to admit knowledge of an act and may lead to a nonchalant attitude toward sin. To ask forgiveness, even though forgiveness is already extended, is to repent, to change, to improve. Acknowledgment states an awareness; forgiveness strengthens the relationship.

In confessing privately to another person whom you have wronged, the following guidelines may prove helpful:

1. Be sensitive in your timing. Choose a time when the two of you can talk with minimal interruption and distraction. Set aside ample time so that the conversation is not hurried.
2. Be selective in your wording. Avoid the language of pride and accusation. Your purpose is to admit *your* failure, sin, or deception, not the person's you're confessing to. If he or she is also guilty, let the Holy Spirit do the convicting.
3. Consider including a third party. If your confession deals with a major issue (especially sins of a moral nature), you may find it helpful to have another party present at your discussion. This person should be someone whose confidence you both can trust and one who is able to offer biblical counsel. He or she can help direct the conversation and prevent the breakdown of communication.
4. Be specific in the naming of your sin(s) and accept full responsibility for your actions. Avoid vague terminology.

5. Do not confess in stages or the person may wonder, "What's coming next?" While the wound is open, complete the surgery.

6. Give the other person time to deal with your confession. Realize that he or she may have to work through the process of forgiveness and may wait to see if your repentance is genuine. Remember that forgiveness is not a right, but an undeserved blessing.[5]

While private confession has been practiced faithfully through the years, public confession seems to be regaining popularity. Practiced in biblical times (see sidebar), it has also seen resurgence prior to and in the midst of genuine revival. However, some caution needs to be offered related to the public confession of sin. Time spent in such sharing must be supervised. The leaders of Ezra's day allowed for it but knew when to stop it and turn the people to rejoicing. Likewise, public confession must be accompanied by and be true to the Bible (Acts 19:18–20; James 5:16). Further, these declarations must be accompanied by true repentance and determination to follow through with a changed lifestyle. The Old Testament covenant was one means by which this has been carried out in the past (2 Chron. 14–16; 23:12–21; 34–35; Ezra 10). Always, public acknowledgment of sin must be done with propriety and sensitivity. Let the circle of the sin define the circle of the confession and let no one confess the sins of others in public.[6]

During a scheduled forty-five minute chapel service that lasted seven hours, public confession of sin by students at Southwestern Baptist Seminary was the predominant feature of the day. Students lined up to share with fellow students. One student from a southern state confessed that he grew up isolated from African-Americans and was taught that they were not equal to him. He went to a predominately white university,

Some "public confession" scriptures:

1 Kings 8:28–53
Ezra 9:3–10:1
Nehemiah 1:4–11
Nehemiah 9
Daniel 9:3–23

and seminary had thrust him for the first time in his life into the company of black students. As he confessed his feelings, a black student came to the front and jumped onto the stage. He was not there to retaliate, but to embrace and forgive. Several days later I learned that these two students, one white, the other black, were now prayer partners. Public confession, followed by public forgiveness, resulted in the unity of two believers and the increased power of intercession. It also demonstrated God's purpose for confession and restoration to a chapel full of seminary students.

The next letter, *T*, denotes Thanksgiving, as demonstrated in 1 Thessalonians 5:18 and 1 Timothy 2:1. Thanksgiving is expressing gratitude for what God has done, is doing, and will do. Thus, we should thank God for what has been done—God saved us, sustained us, provided for us, and brought us to this place. We should thank God for what is presently being done—God is teaching us, strengthening us, and equipping us. And we should thank God for what will be done—God will direct us, protect us, and take us to heaven. Thanksgiving grows by expressing it. We may give thanks for those blessings God has given us without our asking and for those blessings we've received in response to our prayer requests. One of the marks of Christian growth is the decrease in prayer petitions for self and the increase in thankfulness for what God has done, is doing, and will do.

One night in 1860 Ed Spencer was awakened from his dormitory bed by shouts of fellow students. "Shipwreck!" they cried. "Right off the shore of Winnetka!" As a student at Garrett Theological Seminary, Ed lived close to Lake Michigan. Though shipwrecks were not uncommon then, this was an excursion ship with four hundred people on board. Ed jumped up, dressed hurriedly, and ran the three miles north to Winnetka. It was a stormy night and the lake was unsettled. A strong undertow discouraged many would-be rescuers. But Ed, a young man studying to become a Methodist minister, was a strong swimmer. He plunged into the chilly waters and began pulling people to the shore. For six hours he swam back and forth, battling huge waves that swept over him as well as bits of the ship's debris which cut and bruised him. By dawn, Ed had made fifteen trips, bringing in fifteen people.

As he rested by a warm fire, he heard someone shout, "There are two more out there!" Though exhausted, Ed dove into the surf again, barely able to reach the man and woman who were clinging desperately to a piece of wreckage. He brought them both in and collapsed on the beach. In all, 287 people drowned and 98 survived, 17 of whom were rescued singlehandedly by a theological student who was finally carried off the beach to a hospital. Years later, as an old man with white hair, Ed was interviewed in Los Angeles. Asked if he remembered anything in particular about the rescue, Ed replied, "Only this: of the seventeen people I saved, not one of them thanked me."

The few who sincerely give thanks are represented by the one Samaritan leper who returned to thank Jesus for his healing (Luke 17:11-19). There were ten lepers who cried for mercy and ten who were healed. Ten lepers also went on their way back into the mainstream of healthy life. Only one returned to give thanks. Sad are the words of our Lord, "Were there not ten cleansed? But the nine— where are they?" (Luke 17:17). I wonder if Jesus is not still looking for the majority to express their thankfulness.

Beyond adoration, confession, and thanksgiving, the *S* denotes Supplication/Petition as demonstrated in Matthew 7:7-11 where Jesus encouraged the disciples to keep on asking. Petition is that dimension of prayer which asks God for specific personal things, to meet a need on the part of self. Supplication is not the prayer of a person opening heaven's doors to release God's answer; rather, it is the prayer of a person opening the life door to receive answers already appropriated by God. In other words, supplication prompts God to give us what God has already set aside for us.

Specifically, our Lord taught people to pray for certain things for themselves:

- for that which ministers to physical well being (Matt. 6:11; Luke 11:3)
- for deliverance from temptation or trial (Matt. 6:13; Luke 11:4)
- for the fullness of the Holy Spirit (Luke 11:13)

Other personal requests were made, such as:

- Peter's petition for safety (Matt. 14:30)
- The thief's petition for salvation (Luke 23:42)
- Zechariah's prayer for a son (Luke 1:13).

Are we then limited in what we may ask of God in supplication prayer? Not at all. The Bible is clear that we may ask for anything (Matt. 21:22; John 14:14). Just as in the human family, so in the heavenly family, anything that is a concern of the child is a concern of the loving Father. Again, as in the human family so in the divine, regardless of the petitions of the children, the loving Father responds for the good of the whole family rather than for the selfishness of one child.

Most families have experienced circumstances where to yield to one member's request would disrupt the unity and orderliness of the entire family. However, no child should ever be discouraged from asking, either in the human family or in God's family.

"In everything by prayer and supplication with thanksgiving let your requests be made known to God" (Phil. 4:6). But let's explore this private dimension of prayer further. The prayer-shaped disciple knows how to pray alone.

5. Privacy:
Where One Is Gathered

The stress of interpersonal relationships demands that we spend time alone with God. The anxiety of constant exposure to people was evidenced recently by a news story indicating that the Tokyo City Zoo would be closed for two days each month. The law became necessary because zoo officials discovered the animals were showing signs of extreme emotional distress due to constant exposure to the public. Likewise, there are times in our lives when the "zoo" needs to be closed for a period of time.

Our Lord felt it necessary in his public ministry to frequently withdraw from the crowds for time alone with the Father. Jesus demonstrated to us one of the secrets of interpersonal ministry. Private time with the Father is a key to effective prayer.

Praying alone and in private is biblical. Isaac went into the fields to pray and meditate. Jacob remained on the eastern bank of the Brook Jabbok. Moses hid in the clefts of the rocks on Mt. Horeb. Elijah withdrew to the lonely crest of Mt. Carmel. Daniel remained on the banks of Hiddekel. On one occasion Paul arranged to go by land while his associates traveled by ship, perhaps to use the time alone for prayer (Acts 20:13). John, though not of his own will, prayed alone on Patmos.

Because it is just you alone, there are self-restraints required in private prayer. You will not have the support of another Christian or a group of Christians to hold you accountable to the task of praying. Therefore, more self-control will be needed. Consider the following disciplines of private prayer:

1. The discipline of time. In a survey by *Leadership* magazine it was discovered that 34 percent felt time was the greatest hindrance to private prayer.[1] A similar survey was conducted by *Evangelical Missions Quarterly*, which reported out of 390 missionaries surveyed, 11 percent spent less than an average of five minutes per day in prayer. Sixty percent spent between eleven and thirty minutes daily in prayer.[2] In contrast consider Andrew Bonar, who wrote in his diary, "I work more than I pray. I must at once return, through the Lord's strength, to not less than three hours per day spent in prayer and meditation upon the Word."[3] Or consider Adoniram Judson, who said:

> Arrange thy affairs, if possible, so that thou canst leisurely devote two or three hours every day not merely to devotional exercises but to the very act of secret prayer and communication with God. Endeavor seven times a day to withdraw from business and company and lift thy soul to God in private retirement.[4]

The difference between these two great prayer warriors' practice and ours is not one of inherent nature. It is simply that they took time to ponder God and to study him in an act of supreme attention. We are too greatly overrun with our own trivial pursuits to find leisure for such time of spiritual pondering.

As to how to spend the disciplined time alone with God, Dick Eastman has helped us by dividing prayer into twelve categories. He suggests that "'keep watch with Me for one hour'" (Matt. 26:40) be divided into twelve equal parts (see sidebar).

The reference to "scripture praying" in the sidebar may need a further explanation. In his book *Touch the World Through Prayer*,

Wesley Duewel suggests ten ways to use scripture in seeking to make your prayer time more effective:

1. Begin your regular prayer time with God's Word.
2. Apply to your life what you read.
3. Personalize scripture passages during your prayer time.
4. Bathe your soul in scripture to increase your faith.
5. Memorize verses of scripture which will be useful in prayer.
6. Use scripture in praising and worshiping the Lord.
7. Use scripture to confess your unworthiness.
8. Use scripture prayers and prayer expressions.
9. Claim the Bible promises when you pray.
10. Use scripture to rebuke Satan.[5]

Daniel gave us an example of the discipline of time: "Three times a day he got down on his knees and prayed, giving thanks to his God" (Dan. 6:10 NIV). Daniel set an appointment with God and kept it faithfully. Whether early in the morning or late at night, you must set a time and with spiritual discipline remain faithful to it.

2. The discipline of place. *Leadership* magazine reported that 42 percent of those surveyed prayed in their office while 20 percent prayed at home and 10 percent at church.[7] Jesus not only had a favorite time for private prayer (early in the morning), but was always able, even in the midst of his travels, to find "a secluded place" (Mark 1:35) for prayer. In the busiest seasons of his life, Jesus would rob himself of needed rest in order that he might have the quiet and unhurried place for prayer. For Jesus the place was

Twelve ways to spend an hour in prayer:[6]

Praising (Ps. 63:3)
Waiting (Ps. 46:10)
Confessing (Ps. 139:23)
Scripture praying (Jer. 23:29)
Watching (Col. 4:2)
Interceding (1 Tim. 2:1–2)
Petitioning (Matt. 7:7)
Thanksgiving (1 Thess. 5:18)
Singing (Ps. 100:2)
Meditating (Josh. 1:8)
Listening (Eccles. 5:2)
Praising (Ps. 52:9)

not as important as the purpose, namely to get away from the routine and the interruptions and spend time alone with the Father. There are no sacred places, just places that become sacred because of what happens there between a person and God. It will be of great benefit to you if you can designate a location for private prayer. If you are not able to do this, then, like Jesus, you should seek some temporary "secluded place."

3. The discipline of mind. You must learn how to relax without your mind shifting into neutral. Perhaps concentrating on a written prayer list will help. Try listening as well as speaking to God. *The Evangelical Missions Quarterly* reported that out of 257 missionaries surveyed, sixty-six percent cited "mind wandering" during prayer as a frequent occurrence. Only one said it never happened to him.[8] You and I must discipline our mind to concentrate. W. E. Sangster says:

> Let no beginner in prayer abandon the privilege because of mind wandering. It can be conquered. A brisk, live imagination and a resolute will cannot be denied. Even though, in the early stages, the precious minutes tick away and all the time seems spent in bringing the mind back from its wanderings and fixing it again on prayer, they are not moments lost. Such discipline will exercise the muscles of the will, and the day will dawn when the sweetest meditation and the most earnest prayer will be possible even amid distraction.[9]

4. The discipline of continuation. While in public prayer there needs to be an "amen" to indicate to others that the prayer is finished, in private prayer you never need to say "amen." Let the communication continue beyond the special time and apart from the special place. Allow the Lord to continue communication with you throughout the day. It is like parents wanting to stay in touch with their children. How often in your childhood did one of your parents call your name and when you responded they said, "I just wanted to know if you were okay"? The discipline of continuation allows God to continue communication with us.

5. The discipline of organization. Keep a prayer list, diary, or notebook. List the names of people and issues you are praying for. Your list might include government leaders, church leaders, missionaries, friends, and specific needs among associates and colleagues. Record answers to prayers and items of praise. Since no one else is involved, you will need to employ your own discipline of organization.

Even as there are special disciplines required in private prayer, so there are special benefits.

One benefit is that it affords us the ability to live *in* a sinful world while not being *of* that world. Francis DeSales called prayer and private devotion a "spiritual nosegay." In the seventeenth century one could hardly stand to walk down the streets of Europe because of the stench coming from open sewers. The ladies of that day learned to carry a small bouquet of sweet-smelling flowers with them when they went walking. As they approached an open sewer they would simply lift the flowers to their nose. The aroma would offset the stench of the open sewers. These bouquets of flowers were called nosegays. Thus, prayer becomes the spiritual nosegay allowing us the freedom to live in this sinful world with all of its stench while not being fully a part of this world.

Another result of private prayer is a growing concern for other people. It is impossible to pray for a particular person day after day and not become increasingly concerned for him. Likewise, it is impossible to pray for an institution or organization on a regular basis without becoming increasingly concerned for it.

Recently, I had a series of four surgeries for skin cancer in a thirty-six day period. The procedures included not only removal of the cancer and its roots, but some rather detailed facial reconstruction and plastic surgery. Many friends and associates prayed for me during the first surgery. Cards, phone calls, and e-mail poured in from around the world. By the second surgery, the attention I received was a bit less and by the fourth surgery, I received almost no notice other than that of family and close associates. I had to ask myself questions about some of these pray-ers. Did they really continue to pray, but their concern waned? Or did they cease to pray as the days went by? Or did they continue to pray, but just ceased to communicate with me? I'd like to believe the latter. However, I fear that many ceased to pray, since continued private prayer creates a growing concern for those who are the objects of our intercession. And in every other area of life, a growing concern leads to growing communication.

Private prayer also affords you opportunity to lead by example before those who don't practice it. There is no better motivation to faithful intercession than to see a respected believer consistently modeling the practice of private prayer. I was greatly influenced early in my ministry by the discipline of a supervisor, W. F. Howard. In addition to his own practice, he continually recommended both books on prayer and books of prayers as aids to my own practice. I, in turn, tried to be an example for others. I learned, however, if you appear more spiritual than those whom you are trying to influence, the result will likely be negative. A quiet, humble model is best.

As an enhancement to personal prayer, one person I know takes an occasional private retreat. Because we are active people, we tend to think of quiet time, especially extended quiet time, as wasted. Active spiritual work seems more important than praying. On an occasion, perhaps even as often as once per month, set aside a full day or a portion of a day for a private prayer retreat. This will allow for an extended time of private communication with God as well as give a fresh perspective on your relationship with others.

Why spend an extended time in private prayer? First, the more time we spend with someone, the better acquainted we become. Brief periods of fellowship lead to shallow relationships. Quantity time leads to quality relationships. Second, extended time in prayer affords you ample opportunity for personal renewal and reflection. The longer we communicate with God, the better we understand ourselves. The more we look at Jesus, the more clearly we see ourselves. Third, it will allow greater time of intercession for others. Brief times of prayer cut short the amount of attention we can give to others and lessen the time spent wrestling in prayer for others' needs. Finally, it offers deeper preparation for service. A call to share is a call to prepare. The extent of our effective sharing in service will be largely determined by the depth of our preparation in prayer.

There are several factors that must be considered when planning such a retreat. Choose a place where there will be no interruptions either by telephone or in person. Often the outdoors provides an appropriate setting. You might also make use of public places such as parks. If you have the financial resources, travel-related places may also be used effectively. A friend of mine spends a day in a nearby motel room. This often provides the privacy needed. My own personal preference is to buy a train ticket and rent a sleeping car compartment. When I arrive at my destination, I fulfill my responsibilities and then I am able to have another private prayer retreat during my return trip. Unfortunately, tight schedules and crowded calendars allow for less and less of this travel-prayer luxury.

Also give attention to the time and the physical preparation. Private prayer retreats might range from a portion of a day to an overnight experience to an extended vacation. Whatever the length of time, someone should be notified as to your location in case of an emergency, and you should begin this time rested. Necessary interruptions such as meals (assuming one is not fasting during the private prayer retreat) should be arranged in such a way so as not to distract from the purpose of the retreat.

Resources necessary for an effective retreat include a Bible, a concordance, and a note pad with several pens or pencils. A hymnal or favorite devotional book might be desirable. Don't forget your prayer list. I've also found it helpful to take an alarm clock. If I must end the retreat at a particular time or interrupt it for a particular function, I simply set the alarm and don't look again at the clock until it sounds.

During the retreat itself, activities might include personal prayer, intercessory prayer, meditation, praise, singing, and writing down impressions and future plans. Lorne Sanny suggests we divide the prayer time into three parts:

- waiting on the Lord (Isa. 40:31; Ps. 27:14;. 62:5)
- praying for others (Ps. 125:4)
- praying for self (Ps. 119:18)[10]

A private prayer retreat can be a stimulating time of spiritual refreshment as well as an incentive to more effective ministry and service. Prior to our Lord's public ministry, he spent forty days in the wilderness. One might well define this forty-day period as a private prayer retreat in preparation for ministry. Consider that for forty days—more than a month—Jesus was alone on a wilderness retreat, learning what makes a paradise of desert places. And when he was made ready by the Father, his ministry began.

In his ministry Jesus mentioned the prayer "closet" (Matt. 6:6 KJV). The word rendered "closet" signified originally a storeroom and has the same root word as the word "to cut" or "divide." It may have referred to a sectioning-off of a corner of the large room in which the family lived. In that private place supplies were kept for the needs of the family. While this word eventually came to be used for any place of privacy, the "supply room" would also speak to the storehouse of God's resources available to us through private prayer.

Recently I was sitting at my office desk, but I wasn't accomplishing any work. A major personal decision was weighing heavy on my mind. I could not concentrate on the papers in front of me. A phone call came and I went through the motions, hardly aware of the conversation. My secretary informed me that a student desired to talk with me. I met with the student but only vaguely recall the content of the conversation. Finally, I gave up all attempts to concentrate on anything other than the issue that was dominating my thinking. I got up from my desk and went to my prayer bench. This little kneeling rail occupies only a small portion of my office, but its presence is highly significant. It is my "prayer closet," a tiny section of the office cut off from the rest, an island of solitude in a sea of activity. There, in that private moment, I petitioned God on behalf of the current issue. When I arose, I not only had peace, I had power for the remainder of the day, an added resource. While I go to that bench-shaped prayer closet at the beginning of each day, I also find times when a visit there gives impetus for the hours at hand.

A little poem entitled "A Call to Prayer," by Clinton Scollard, summarizes the beauty and the blessings of private prayer:

> Let us put by some hour of every day
> For holy things!—Whether it be when dawn
> Peers through the window-pane, or when the noon
> Flames, like a burnished topaz, in the vault,
> Or when the thrush pours in the ear of eve
> Its plaintive monody; some little hour
> Wherein to hold rapt converse with the soul,
> From sordidness and self sanctuary,
> Swept by the winnowing of unseen wings,
> And touched by the White Light Ineffable!

Now you have identified your heavenly and earthly prayer partners, acknowledged God's responses to your prayers, considered prayer's basic ingredients, and explored how to pray alone. Perhaps it is time to look at the supreme model for praying—the Lord's Prayer.

6. The Lord's Prayer:
Model Glue

The model prayer, according to Matthew, begins with the statement, "After this manner" (Matt. 6:9 KJV). This is a model, not a mimic. It is not to be repeated in a meaningless way. In Matthew's account, Jesus has just said, "Do not use meaningless repetition" (Matt. 6:7). The fact that this prayer is repeated in Luke 11:2–4 with different words indicates this prayer was not given by Jesus to be memorized and repeated as a ritual. In Matthew's account, it is given as a part of the Sermon on the Mount. In Luke's account, it is given in response to the disciples' request, "Teach us to pray" (Luke 11:1). While there is nothing wrong with memorizing this prayer, it was given as a model rather than as a repeated ritualistic part of worship. If understood it will hold us in a glue-like grip to biblical praying. It includes the Lord's invocation, requests, and doxology.

Comparing Matthew's and Luke's versions of The Lord's Prayer provides the following parallel:

Matthew 6:9-13	Luke 11:2-4
"Our Father who is in heaven,	"Father,
hallowed be Your name.	hallowed be Your name.
Your kingdom come.	Your kingdom come.
Your will be done, on earth as it is in heaven.	
Give us this day our daily bread.	Give us each day our daily bread.
And forgive us our debts, as we also have forgiven our debtors.	And forgive us our sins, for we ourselves also forgive everyone who is indebted to us.
And do not lead us into temptation, but deliver us from evil.	And lead us not into temptation."
For Yours is the kingdom and the power and the glory forever. Amen."	

This prayer has been treasured by believers across the centuries. In the early church, personalities such as Origen, Gregory of Nyssa, Tertullian, Cyril of Jerusalem, and Cyprian all wrote expositions of the prayer, as did Augustine. Dante expounded its significance in the eleventh canto of his *Purgortorio*. Luther gave several expositions of the true meaning of the prayer to the heirs of the Protestant Reformation.

Introducing his book of sermons during World War II, when many cities were being devastated by air raids, the German pastor Helmut Thielicke wrote:

> The Lord's Prayer is truly the prayer that spans the world; the world of everyday trifles and universal history, the world with its hours of joy and bottomless anguish, the world of citizens and soldiers, the world of monotonous routine, sudden terrible catastrophe, the world of carefree children and at the same time of problems that can shatter grown men.[1]

Still in our day, this prayer is available in the simplicity with which we teach children and in the complexity with which we challenge the scholar. Some have called it a school of prayer. Indeed, it is both a pre-school and a graduate school. This prayer has been called, "the single most important part of Jesus' teaching on prayer and the most characteristic prayer of Christians from then on."[2]

The Lord's Invocation—Matthew 6:9a

Father. This is the first time in the Bible that God is called Father in prayer. No one knew, until Jesus taught them, that they could come to God as "Father." Jesus prayed "Father" more than seventy times. The only exception in the prayer life of Jesus is when, from the cross, he prayed, "My God," and this prayer was followed by the seventh statement from the cross which began with "Father." God is Father in two senses. The Greek word *Pater* means responsible for life or image. Thus, fatherhood was not necessarily involved. The child may have never even seen the father. In this sense God is Father of all creation. All people are made in God's image. The second sense in which God is father is "Fatherhood"—meaning love, intimacy, confidence—in God's image. While some never know the Father and others know only of the Father, Christians have been adopted as children of the Father (Gal. 4:4-7; Rom. 8:15-17). We are joint heirs with Christ and with him we celebrate God's fatherhood by calling on God as "father."

Thomas Hardy asked what was the use of prayer when we have no one to whom to pray except "the dreaming, dark, dumb Thing; that turns the handles of the idle Show." But we do have one to whom we pray—one who is our Father. He is not father goose, not father nature, not father Santa Claus, but Father God.

Our Father. Most of the world of Jesus' day worshiped gods that were distant, remote, and fearful. Even the Jews spoke of the god of "that mountain" or the god who dwelled in the tabernacle. Two major philosophies of Jesus' day were Stoicism and Epicureanism. The Stoics believed the major attribute of God was described by the Greek word *apatheia,* meaning the inability to express feeling. If one feels love, one would also feel hurt. If one feels joy, one would also feel pain. Since they did not believe God could feel hurt or pain, they assumed that God could feel nothing. They were "apathetic." The Epicureans believed the supreme quality of God was described by the Greek word *ataraxia,* meaning serenity, or calm. If God got involved with the world, then God would lose the quality of calmness. Thus, they believed that God was not involved with the world.

The fact that Jesus said "Our" Father was against the thinking of his day. Because he identified the personal nature of God, two things are settled: (1) Our relationship to God, and (2) our relationship to God's family.

In heaven. This is not a reference to a geographical sphere. God is Spirit. God inhabits the eternal. God is worshiped by angels. This phrase indicates the *otherness* of God versus the *closeness* of God represented by the word "our." A balance is found. Since my Father is "in heaven," I can expect such gifts as can come from heaven. All that comes from heaven will make life more heavenly.

This invocation then means: "Father," which settles the hopelessness of the worldly "Our," which settles the selfishness of man (not I, me, or my, but our); and "heaven," which settles the resources (earth is limited but not heaven).

The Lord's Requests—Matthew 6:9b-13

The first three requests, related to God, correspond to the first four commandments. The second three, related to man, correspond to commandments five through ten.

Requests Related to God
God's Name

Hallowed. The Greek word is *hagiazo.* It means to sanctify, to treat as holy, to revere. The word is used twice in the Old Testament, in Isaiah 29:23 and in Ezekiel 36:23. Perhaps the most unusual rendering in an attempt to fully define the word "Hallowed" came from Edward Harwood in a translation entitled, *A Liberal Translation of the New Testament: Being an Attempt to Translate the Sacred*

Writings with the Same Freedom, Spirit, and Elegance with which other English Translations from the Greek Classics have lately been Executed, dated 1768. Harwood's translation of this first part of the Lord's Prayer reads:

O, thou great governor and parent of universal nature—who manifesteth thy glory to the blessed inhabitants of heaven—may all thy rational creatures in all the parts of thy boundless dominion be happy in the knowledge of thy existence and providence, and celebrate thy perfections in a manner most worthy of thy nature and perfective of their own.[3]

Hallowing the name of Jesus is important not only as it relates to prayer, but also as we learn that every significant spiritual awakening since Pentecost had in its beginning stages a return to the holiness of God. As you become broken and aware of the sinful nature, you tend to return to God in prayer. Praying to God must be done as to one whose name is hallowed.

Thy Name. Prayer begins with *who* God is and continues with *what* God is. In Biblical times, the name stood for much more than it does today. Often the name represented the character of the person. Examples of this may be found in Psalm 9:10, Psalm 20:7, and John 17:6. The Hebrews had created a new name for God because of the reverence for his name. Since they would not speak the name of Yahweh, they took the consonants of Yahweh and the vowels of Adonai to make the word Jehovah. Thus, they would not have to dishonor God's name by speaking it through their sinful lips.

Jesus' further teaching hallowed the name of God. Since you can't separate the name from the person, Jesus is saying that God must be recognized as holy. Thus, the petition related to God's name is one that speaks of holiness. The first word spoken to Moses on Mt. Horeb had to do with him standing on holy ground, in God's holy presence (Gen. 3:5). Again, in Isaiah 6:3, Isaiah in the temple recognized the threefold holiness of God. On April 12, 1892, at the funeral service for Alfred Lord Tennyson, the hymn "Holy, Holy,

Holy" was appropriately sung because it was Tennyson who penned the famous line, "More things are wrought by prayer than this world dreams of." In prayer we call upon the name of a hallowed and holy God.

God's Kingdom:

Kingdom. This is the Greek word *basileia,* meaning rule or reign. One must approach this word like a child with a bucket standing before the mighty seas, wondering how to fit the seas into the bucket. God's kingdom needs to come in the individual life, in the family, in the church, in the country, and in the world.

Earthly kingdoms have come and gone, but God's kingdom is eternal. The great Pastor R. G. Lee described the kingdoms of this world and their fall as follows:

> Saddened we are to think of how Babylon—glorious and great— became a vermin-infested, animal-prowling jungle. Sobered we are when we think that ancient Rome with her close-meshed code of laws and her victorious legions became as a branchless tree, dishonorable, fruitless. Regret assails our minds when we think of how ancient Greece, with all her art and philosophy and athletic prowess and philosophers, became a molded crust in history's garbage can. Saddened we are when we read history's book and learn how ancient Egypt with all her wealth and wonders, became a shabby sexton of splendid tombs. And we are awed into fear and trembling for other nations of our world today, when we remember ancient Spain, with her piratical ships that harassed all seas and filled the nation's coffers with gold, felt the hand of God's retributive Providence—and became a lousy, drowsy beggar watching a broken clock.[4]

Thy Kingdom. So common was this idea in prayer that Jews in our Lord's day prayed in the words of the *Kaddish*: "May his kingdom be established in your lifetime." The emphasis here is upon "thy" rather than "my." When God invades your life, priorities go contrary to all modern teaching. The world teaches us to look out for and promote self. This prayer speaks of "thy Name," "thy Kingdom," and "thy Will."

Thus, the Kingdom is to come in three tenses: (1) in the past tense, when we changed our citizenship from earth to heaven through conversion. We were at that point no longer of this world, but beginning to look for a city whose builder and maker is God; (2) in the present tense, in that we are living out that heavenly citizenship now through commitment to Christ and fellowship through his church; and (3) in the future tense, in that one day our citizenship will be fully realized through the consummation of his eternal Kingdom. Noted theologian Karl Barth voiced it this way:

> We pray for the removal of this covering which now conceals all things, as the cloth which covers this table. The table is underneath ... But you do not see it. You have only to remove the cloth to see it. We pray in order that the covering which still veils the reality of the kingdom may be removed, in order that the reality of everything already changed in Jesus Christ may be made visible.[5]

God's Will

In the beginning there was only one will—God's perfect will. The Bible introduces us to Satan who had rebelled against God (Gen. 3; Isa. 14:12-14) and broke the harmony of the universe, thus presenting a second will—Satan's imperfect will. First there was one will, then two, then, with God's creation of human life, four wills, then eight wills, then thousands and millions of wills, including ours. The only way earth can experience heaven is when God's will is done on earth, because it is already being done in heaven. The literal Greek work for will means whatever you wish to happen, let it happen. In other words, as it is in heaven, so let it be on earth. This is not a request for God to take us immediately to heaven, but to bring heaven through us to the world. We are not asking for escape but for victory, not for rescue but for reinforcement.

G. H. Morrison raises the following question:

> (Whether or not) there is ever joy in prayer when men come to the Father wanting their own way. That joy is born when they have learned to come wanting nothing but the way of God. It is then that there comes sweet peace into the soul. It is then that we learn

that no evil can befall us. It is then that we find, through fair and foul, that underneath are the everlasting arms. And this is such a wonderful discovery, in a life so difficult and intricate as ours, that it brings the ransomed of the Lord to Zion with songs and everlasting joy upon their heads.[6]

God's will is that none should perish (2 Pet. 3:9). However, people are perishing without Christ. Therefore we must pray all the more "Thy will be done" because it is not being done.

God's will is done in heaven by angels (Ps. 103:20). There it is done unwaveringly for there is no discussion or debate in heaven. There it is done completely for there are no alternatives in heaven. There it is done sincerely, for angels are eager for the next command. There it is done willingly, for there is only one will in heaven.

On earth, God's will is comprehensive (Eph. 1:9–11; Isa. 14:24–27; Jer. 51:29), compassionate (Matt. 23:37; 2 Pet. 3:9), and complementary. We tend to judge the effectiveness of our prayer life by how much time we spend in prayer or how well we word our prayers. True judgment is whether something is in accordance with God's will.

Requests Related to Man

We have seen *who* God is and *what* God is; now we will see what God *does*. The following three requests allow God to be glorified: in bread (physical), in debt (mental/social), and in temptation (spiritual). Even as Jesus grew in wisdom, stature, favor with God, and favor with man, we are to grow in prayer by seeing God glorified in each of these areas.

Man's Sustenance—Bread:
Give us. Matthew's account uses the Greek word *dos,* meaning to give in one act, while Luke's account uses the Greek word *didon,* meaning to give continuously. Whether God gives in one act or continuously, the giving is because God is owner (Ps. 50:10; Hag. 2:8) and because God has resources to give (Phil. 4:19). The

certainty that God will give was expressed by Methodist evangelist Sam Jones when he reportedly said, "God will take care of His own even if He has to put the angels on half rations." The psalmist says he has never seen the righteous begging for bread (Ps. 37:25). Note that we are not to ask that God "spoon feed" us. The fact that God gives us bread carries with it a responsibility on our part to do what we can to produce and distribute more bread for others, since "Give us" does not invite idleness. While the gifts of God of daily necessities honor the resourceful work of humanity, our work is never enough without divine help.

Note also that bread is to be given to *us,* not to *me* individually. This stresses again the plural nature of this prayer to be prayed by the family of God.

Bread. This simple yet profound request is described by T. H. Robinson as follows:

> The circle in which Jesus and his disciples had always lived was one in which employment was uncertain and actual living precarious. Bread for the morrow is a problem of ever-present urgency, and the natural thing is for man in communion with his Father to mention this as a pressing need.[7]

Bread here represents all man's physical needs. It may also refer to spiritual needs. This connection between the physical and spiritual is alluded to here and in the hymn text by Mary A. Lathbury:

> Break Thou the Bread of Life,
> Dear Lord, to me,
> as thou didst break the loaves
> beside the sea;
> Beyond the sacred page
> I seek thee, Lord,
> My spirit pants for thee,
> O living word.

Note also that Jesus asked only for bread, not for life's luxuries. He did not even ask for butter or jelly. Our prayer requests and petitions should be only for that which we need, not for luxuries. Jesus criticized those who obsess on nonessentials (Matt. 6:19–21, 25).

This day. This keeps us in daily contact with and dependence upon God. The Greek word used for "this day" is *epiousios.* The idea is used only here and in Luke's account and is used nowhere in Greek literature. This leads us to conclude that the word may have been a coined word. The idea of "this day" relates to Exodus 16:14, when the manna was provided morning by morning, and 2 Kings 25:30 which says, "Every day a portion, all the days of thy life." It might also be noted that the God who gives us the day also gives us the resources for the day.

Thus, to summarize, the substance of this request is "bread"; the source of this request is "God"; the supplication of this request is "give"; the seekers in this request are "us"; and the schedule of this request is "this day."

Man's Forgiveness

Following the request that asks God to give comes a request asking God to *for*give. When we remember the resources out of which God gives to us, then we recognize how little we deserve to receive from those vast resources and we cry out for forgiveness.

Forgive. This word means "to send away," "divorce," "let go." The head of a large British hospital has said, "I could dismiss half my patients tomorrow if they could be assured of forgiveness." [8]

Debts. The Greek word is *opheilema.* It is used only two other times in the Bible (Rom. 4:4; Deut. 24:10) and on both occasions has reference to monetary debt. However, the word may also have a broader meaning and refer to moral debts against individuals and the community.

In Luke's account, the word is not *opheilema* but rather *hamartia.* This word is translated "sins." It was not originally an ethical word, but a word meaning "missing the mark." In this sense, sin is missing the mark. These two words are not radically different in their meaning and the difference between Matthew's and Luke's account of the Lord's Prayer may well be attributed to the fact that Jesus spoke the prayer not in Greek but in Aramaic. Both Matthew and Luke translated the prayer into Greek for their writing.

Some early translations use the word "trespasses." This is unexplainable and, linguistically speaking, there is little justification for this translation. Whether translated debts or sins, the fact is man owes a debt to God because God has been set apart and has exchanged for us the freedom of choice for the slavery of sin. That fact has put man in debt to God and alienated him from God through sin. As A. C. Dixon said:

> Our sins against God are all debts overdue, and we are bankrupt. We owe ten thousand talents and have not a penny to pay. It is a debt to the justice of God, and the love of God in Jesus Christ makes full payment for all who will confess their sins and gratefully accept the payment.[9]

In my spiritual bankruptcy, Jesus paid my debt. Indeed, what we sometimes sing is true: "I owed a debt I could not pay; He paid a debt He did not owe."

As we forgive. This is a prerequisite to God's forgiveness. Being unwilling to forgive others is like destroying the bridge you yourself must pass over; or the communication lines over which you must receive communication. The connection between human and divine forgiveness runs throughout the New Testament (Matt. 18:23-35; 5:7; Luke 6:37-38; James 2:13). What does it mean to ask God to forgive us when we are unwilling to forgive those who have sinned against us? Luther connects the petition of this prayer with Psalm 109:7: "Let his prayer be counted as sin." Thus, when this Lord's Prayer request is prayed by an unforgiving person, it becomes sin in the sight of God. Indeed, "to come to the Father for ourselves, and at the same time keep the fires of active resentment or passive ill will burning against 'our debtors' is a mockery."[10] It is said that General Oglethorpe once remarked to John Wesley, "I never forgive." Wesley answered, "Then I hope, sir, you never sin."

How often should we forgive? Peter asked Jesus if it was all right to just forgive seven times. No doubt, Peter knew that the law required three times and was patting himself on the back for doubling the law and adding one. Jesus responded that we should forgive another person seventy times seven, which is not a reference to 490 times but a reference to continual forgiveness. Even if taken literally, once you have forgiven someone 490 times, you would surely be in the habit of forgiving. Therefore, let us, "Be kind to one another, tender-hearted, forgiving each other, just as God in Christ also has forgiven you" (Eph. 4:32).

In conclusion this request offers four ideas:

1. The problem—man is sinful needing forgiveness.
2. The provision—God offers forgiveness.
3. The plea—confession of sin is necessary to receive forgiveness.
4. The prerequisite—forgiving others is a prerequisite to God forgiving us.

Man's Temptations

Temptation. The Greek word is *peirasmos*. It is a noun and like the Greek nouns which end in *asmos,* it describes a process. The word may also be defined as trial or test. It refers to a natural process. Temptation is not sin, but rather yielding to temptation is sin. The Bible speaks of two kinds of temptations: (1) God's temptation or testing—God tempted or tested Abraham (Gen. 22:1). Other references to God's temptation are found in Deuteronomy 13:3 and 1 Corinthians 10:13; and (2) Satan's temptation—this is Satan alluring us into sin against God. Satan tempts us through circumstances (Jesus in the wilderness being tempted to take a shortcut to the kingdom), through people (Peter tempting Jesus to avoid the cross), and through human nature (the hunger of Jesus in the wilderness). The temptation of this prayer is not that which comes from God as a test of faith nor that which comes from our own inner lusts; this temptation comes directly from Satan.

Lead us not. We are vulnerable and should avoid at all costs situations that test or tempt our vulnerability. This phrase simply encourages us to ask God to help keep us out of situations in which we are vulnerable to sin. We are to be led out of the power of sin and away from the influence of it. What does James mean by his statement, "Let no man when he is tempted say, I am tempted by God" (James 1:13)? If you continue reading, you will discover that James is really condemning the man who blames his sin upon God.

Deliver us from evil. The New International Version reads "Deliver us from the evil one." The Greek text allows equally for either translation and actually there is very little difference between being delivered from evil and from the source of evil, which is the evil one. The whole purpose of the evil one is to cause an interruption in the fellowship and relationship between God and his children. The evil one is the personification of all that is against God. This final petition looks forward to our final release from this evil world. The anticipation is that the time is coming when all opposition from Satan will be put away forever. When this petition is granted, we shall need nothing more. It is in this context that Paul writes to Timothy, "The Lord will deliver me from every evil deed and will bring me safely to His heavenly kingdom" (2 Tim. 4:18).

This last request of the Lord's Prayer acknowledges three things: (1) the problem of human sin; (2) the inability of the human to adequately cope with this temptation to sin; and (3) the fact that both the problem and the temptation should be turned over to God.

In summary of these three requests John Stott writes:

> A trinitarian Christian is bound to see in these petitions a veiled allusion to the Trinity, since it is through the Father's creation and providence that we receive our daily bread, through the Son's atoning death that we may be forgiven and through the Spirit's indwelling power that we are rescued from the evil one.[11]

The Lord's Doxology—Matthew 6:13

This doxology, which is in most modern translations of the New Testament, did not appear in any of the ancient manuscripts. We include it here for the sake of completeness. It must be noted that this prayer begins and ends with God. This later phrase may have been a doxology that was offered by the congregation in response to the quoting of the Lord's Prayer by the minister. It may be an adaptation of the prayer of David as he looked towards the building of the temple by his son Solomon:

> Yours, O LORD, is the greatness, the power and the glory, the victory and the majesty; for all that is in heaven and in earth is Yours; Yours, is the kingdom O LORD, and You are exalted as head over all. Both riches and honor come from You, and You reign over all. In Your hand is power and might; In Your hand it is to make great and to give strength to all. Now therefore, our God, we thank You and praise Your glorious name (1 Chron. 29:11–13 NKJV).

Kingdom. This is a petition of faith and concludes the prayer by acknowledging that God the Father (of the opening petition) is also God the King. It also acknowledges that we are God's subjects and ought to be obedient to God. In fact, so certain is it that the King of Kings will present the kingdom to the Father and destroy all other authority and power, that to pray "Thy kingdom come" is to also pray "Thine is the kingdom."

Power. The Greek word is *dunamis* from which we receive our words dynamite and dynamic. The prayer ends with the idea that the God who hears our prayer has power through the Holy Spirit to answer our prayer and grant our petition in keeping with divine will. James Stewart, a British preacher, describes this power as follows:

> The concentrated might of arrogant iniquity is puny and pathetic and impotent against the power that took Jesus out of the grave . . . The power which went into action in the raising again of Jesus will never, through the darkest of dark ages, fail nor be discouraged: one day it will resurrect the world.[12]

Glory. The word means reputation or esteem, which is only available through Christ. The prayer begins by acknowledging that God is holy and ends with the reverence of one who stands in the splendor of God's glory.

Speaking in chapel at Southwestern Baptist Theological Seminary in Fort Worth, Texas, former missionary to China, Britt Towery, recalled the following incident related to the model prayer:

> Wang Weifan once pastored a Baptist church in China. He is now an associate dean at the Nanjing Theological Seminary where my wife and I were guest teachers.
>
> Just days after the tragic Tiananmen Massacre of June 4, 1989, I visited with him in the Nanjing Seminary. He told what it was like in the Seminary vespers the night of the Beijing massacre. Everyone at the seminary knew what had happened in Beijing. They also knew the army was around Nanjing, ready to move in if necessary. As they closed the service they prayed aloud the Lord's Prayer. This is very common in China worship services. But when they came to the end without any human urging or direction their voices rose as one, strong and loud, on the last phrase "GUO DU, QUAN BING, RONG YAO, QUAN SHI NI DE ZHI DAO YONG YUAN." ". . . THINE BE THE KINGDOM AND THE POWER AND THE GLORY FOREVER. AMEN." They knew where their security was.[13]

The privilege of praying the Lord's Prayer is matched by the responsibility of living the Lord's lifestyle. An unknown author has described the Lord's Prayer as follows:

> I cannot say "our" if I live only for myself.
>
> I cannot say "Father" if I do not endeavor each day to act like His child.
>
> I cannot say "who art in heaven" if I am laying up no treasures there.
>
> I cannot say "hallowed be thy name" if I am not striving for holiness.
>
> I cannot say "thy Kingdom come" if I am not doing all in my power to hasten that wonderful event.
>
> I cannot say "thy will be done" if I am disobedient to His word.
>
> I cannot say "in earth as it is in heaven" if I'll not serve Him here and now.
>
> I cannot say "give us this day our daily bread" if I am dishonest or seeking things by subterfuge.
>
> I cannot say "forgive us our debts" if I harbor a grudge against anyone.

I cannot say "lead us not into temptation" if I deliberately place myself in its path.

I cannot say "deliver us from evil" if I do not put on the whole armor of God.

I cannot say "thine is the kingdom" if I do not give the King the loyalty due him from a faithful subject.

I cannot attribute to Him "the power" if I fear what men may do.

I cannot ascribe to Him "the glory" if I am seeking honor only for myself.

And I cannot say "forever" if the horizon of my life is bounded completely by time.

PART TWO

The

Prayer-Shaped

Disciple

Prays

Through

The day in which we are living has been called the Golden Age of Communication. The need to communicate with each other around town and around our world has captured our imaginations. We desire to hear and to be heard, to understand one another and to be understood. More information has been generated in the last three decades than in the previous five thousand years. Over four thousand books are published every day. One weekday edition of *The New York Times* includes more information than the average person encountered in an entire lifetime in seventeenth century England. Twenty years ago there were only three hundred on-line databases; now over eight thousand such databases store literally billions of bits of information.

Through the creativity of modern communication, God has been assigned a fax number! According to "Talk of the Town" in *The New Yorker*, the Israeli government's telephone company, Bezek, has provided a special telephone line on which people can fax their prayer requests to God. For no extra charge, prayer requests received are taken to the Wailing Wall in Jerusalem and put in its cracks. The centuries-old tradition of writing prayers on pieces of paper and inserting them in the cracks of the Wailing Wall has now been modernized. An ancient method of communicating with God has been updated.[1]

Basic journalistic courses teach that if one intends to relate all the facts in a given situation, six questions must be asked: who, what, where, when, why, and how.[2] These words, which compose the simple elements of rational communication, are also the same six questions we must ask ourselves about prayer. In so doing, we will see how to pray through the questions and experience further communication with God.

From the time I was nine years old until I graduated from high school, I lived with my family in Houston. I knew it was a large city, but only from the perspective of ground level. After being away for several years, I flew back. The plane circled over the city, waiting for permission to land. From above I gained a new perspective and appreciation for the city of Houston. Likewise, being involved in prayer gives one a "ground-level" perspective. Examining the questions of prayer elevates us to a different perspective, a spiritual overview of prayer as two-way communication.

Having looked at a prayer-shaped disciple praying *with,* we are now ready to look at a prayer-shaped disciple praying *through*— through the communications questions of who, what, where, when, why, and how.

7. The Who Question:
With a Little Help from My Friends

In one moment, I was part of a youth group on my way, with my friends, to a church-sponsored social activity. In the next moment, due to the carelessness of a driver who was under the influence of alcohol, I was singled out as the object of much prayer. For the next nine months, I became a medical experiment. In every other case known to the medical authorities in Houston, a person suffering a broken second vertebra of the neck had been either killed or paralyzed by the injury. I was alive and not paralyzed. In the miraculous healing process that followed I found answers to several "who" questions. I learned that a teenage boy could pray to God and have his prayer heard. I also learned that I had a host of prayer support.

Speaking to the *who* question, Jesus agreed to be present "where two or three have gathered . . . " (Matt. 18:20). Since prayer is two-way communication, there must be persons involved. God cannot pray alone, but if we will communicate, God will respond. It is reported that Charles Spurgeon once said, "Let us meet and pray, and if God doth not hear us, it will be the first time He has broken

His promise."[1] With that assurance let us consider the first of our six communication questions.

When Jesus said, "I am the way, and the truth, and the life; no one comes to the Father but through Me" (John 14:6), he implied that we who are in Christ should pray. When Jesus said, "All things you ask in prayer, believing, you will receive" (Matt. 21:22), he implied that we who communicate in faith should pray. In Mark 11:25 Jesus said, "Whenever you stand praying, forgive, if you have anything against anyone; so that your Father who is in heaven will also forgive you your transgressions." He implied that we who forgive others are freed to pray. John implied when we desire to obey and please God, we should pray: "Whatever we ask we receive from Him, because we keep His commandments and do the things that are pleasing in His sight" (1 John 3:22).

The psalmist implied that those of us with our sins confessed up to date should pray, "If I regard wickedness in my heart, the Lord will not hear" (Ps. 66:18). Said in reverse, when I cease to regard wickedness and confess the sin in my heart, the Lord *will* hear. I will long remember the day that a guest speaker came to our Missions class while I was a student in seminary. Her name was Bertha Smith. This spiritual giant of a woman had been a lifetime missionary in China. Appearing to point her finger right at me, she asked one question of our class: "Young man, are your sins confessed up to this very moment?" I had to admit to myself that I had not thought much about that question, but I confess I have often thought about that question since that frightening experience. With our sins forgiven and as our sins are being forgiven, we ought to pray to God.

The question is often asked as to the effectiveness of prayers offered by nonbelievers. The proper question is not, "Can God hear the prayers of non-Christians?" but, "Is God listening?" Certainly God can hear. God created hearing. Just because one can hear does not necessarily mean that he is listening. The idea that God practices selective listening is seen in John 9:31, "We know that God does not hear sinners," and Isaiah 59:2, "Your iniquities have made a separation between you and your God, and your sins have hidden His face from you, so that He does not hear."

But you say you know nonbelievers who have prayed and seen God respond to their requests. Possibly so. Jesus responded to the requests of nonbelievers, such as a Roman officer (Matt. 8:5–13), a Canaanite woman with a demon possessed daughter (Matt. 15:21–28), and a Samaritan woman at a well side (John 4:1–30). Some might argue that even though these were not Jews, they were believers. Others would speculate that when it appears God responds to nonbelievers, it is in reality God responding to the believers' intercessory prayers on behalf of the nonbelievers. Still others would argue that the only prayer heard by God voiced by a non-Christian is the prayer of repentance and request for salvation.

This is not an easy question, nor one that will be answered to the satisfaction of all. If, however, prayer is to be in the name of Jesus, according to the will of God, and in the power of the Holy Spirit, it seems extremely difficult for a nonbeliever to be heard by God apart from a prayer for salvation. Rather, it increases the responsibility of the believer to intercede for the needs of the unsaved.

While all believers should pray, those whom God has called to vocational ministry should pray all the more. Strangely enough, ministry often preempts prayer—that for which we should be praying consumes the time allotted for prayer. Mary Booth went to India with great expectations for ministry, but after five years she returned home on furlough, disappointed and contemplating no return. While home, she was challenged to return with a different perspective. The placing of prayer as a priority of her ministry and its resulting consequences are reflected in her poem:

> God called me out to work for Him,
> And oh, what joy and love
> Came to my life as I went forth
> To win for Heaven above.
> As time went on I saw the need.
> Gross darkness everywhere,
> So in the forefront of my work
> I supplemented prayer.
> God kept me on to work for Him,
> And day by day I learned

How sacred was my blessed task
As o'er the lost I yearned.
With will and purpose on I toiled,
Oft questioning—what availed
This weary striving day by day?
In winning souls—I failed.
He kept me on, and on I went,
And then there came a day
When all was changed—I put it down
That you might know the way—
He stopped me in my self-planned toil,
And laid my purpose bare,
And I, ashamed, rebuked, went down
In agonizing prayer.
He heard me as I turned to Him,
And He just turned to me,
Took both my hands in His, and said,
"Great victories you shall see.
The secret is for you to know
That what you do and where,
The fundamental work for you
Is prayer, deep prayer, real prayer."
And oh, the victories He has wrought
And oh, the souls He won,
When I have prayed right through to God
He brought them one by one.
Until I look and am amazed,
For prayer has brought release
And now I pray, whatever else,
"Lord, keep me on my knees."
Those who should, should pray.

But who prays for us—not *with* us in the relationship of prayer partners, but *for* us as a prayer support team? Results of recent surveys show that every minister needs a prayer team, covering him or her with intercession. One survey taken among pastors revealed 33 percent of them saying, "Being in the ministry is clearly a hazard to my family." Likewise 33 percent felt burnout within the first five years of ministry. Seventy percent said they did not have someone they would consider a close friend. Seventy-five percent reported a significant crisis due to stress at least once a month in their ministry. So intense is the stress that *National and International Religion Report* recently published an 800-number where ministers could receive encouragement. The need for a prayer support team is crucial for the minister as well as for the lay person.

There are several reasons why spiritual leaders need a prayer support team interceding on their behalf. Consider, first, that leaders have greater responsibility than followers and, thus, are more accountable and more victimized by Satan. Second, spiritual leaders become more frequent victims of spiritual warfare especially as they attempt to lead nonbelievers out of Satan's kingdom and into the kingdom of God. Third, because leaders have higher visibility within the church and to some extent in the world, they have greater potential influence than others. Again, Satan likes to discredit this influence. Thus, spiritual leaders need prayer support teams.

There are historical examples of prayer support teams, ranging from the two older men known as Father Clery and Father Nash who prayed for Charles G. Finney, and the teenagers who prayed for Evan Roberts, to the mother and sister who prayed for Hudson Taylor, to the invalid sister who prayed for William Carey, all the way to the prayer support groups that meet today.

Modern missionaries often send out prayer request letters to persons whom they consider to be their prayer support team. A recent letter from a missionary friend requested and received prayer support from me:

> While home on furlough, I have become convinced that it is essential that I increase my prayer support for the work I will be doing. I greatly appreciate the fervent and effective prayer support which I have had in the past. However, the change in work will simply require greater prayer support for me to have any sort of effective ministry. Therefore, I am looking for a group of prayer warriors who will commit to pray for me during the next four years more intensely and more often than in the past. Information about specific prayer concerns and needs will be sent to this group every four to six weeks, along with updates about prayers answered and praises.

I realize this is a commitment beyond regular prayer for missionaries, so I am asking you to consider this very carefully before answering. If you feel God is leading you in this direction and would like to become a part of this prayer team, please respond back to me as soon as possible.

I hope to have a team of ten to fifteen people committed to pray for me in my new work before I return to Taiwan in late June.[2]

While serving with the Southern Baptist Home Mission Board (now, North American Mission Board), my job as a national consultant in evangelism required that I be away from home an average of sixteen days per month. Shortly after beginning this assignment, I realized that many negative things were happening in our family just prior to my leaving on a trip, while I was gone, and immediately upon my return. Problems seemed to lurk around every travel itinerary. I shared this with a colleague and he informed me that I was undergoing a form of spiritual warfare. Since every trip I made was related to either mass or personal evangelism, my colleague said, "Satan doesn't like what you are doing and he is attacking your family to discourage you. What you need is a group of prayer warriors to intercede for you and your family while you are on the road." I proceeded to write letters to approximately fifty friends and family members, asking them to covenant with me to pray for my family while I was traveling. I agreed to send them a copy of my travel itinerary with a brief description of what I would be doing on each assignment. Approximately half of those written responded that they would agree to pray with me. There was an almost immediate difference once this prayer support began. Not all problems ceased nor did our family become one of perfect harmony, but the difference was measurable and positive, and I thanked God for a prayer support team who would intercede on my behalf.

Having evaluated the *who* question, let us move on to the *what* question of the prayer-shaped disciple.

8: The What Question:
What's on Second

The first summer my son played organized baseball provided many exciting experiences. In an early season game, James hit the ball past the infielders for the first time. He ran to first and then stopped. The coach, fellow players, and parents shouted, "Go to second! Go to second!" James remained on first, facing a question unknown to anyone else. After the game, I asked James why he didn't go to second. He said, "What's second?" The *what* question is important in baseball and in life, and its answers shed light on our circumstances. Don't stop on first. Read on *through* the second question.

A look at the prayer life of Jesus tells us that he prayed for:

*   forgiveness and daily sustenance (Matt. 6:9–13; Luke 11:2–24)
*   his disciples both then and now (John 17:1–26)
*   and himself and the Kingdom of God (Matt. 26:36–48)

The only "prayer request" which Jesus gave his church was to pray for harvest (Matt. 9:35–38).

Furthermore, Jesus taught his disciples to pray for:

- those who were ill (Mark 7:32–35; Matt. 10:1; 12:15)
- the children (Matt. 19:13)
- their fellow disciples and co-workers (Luke 6:12–13; 24:50; John 17:10)
- those who were persecuting followers of Jesus (Matt. 5:44; Luke 23:21, 34)
- and laborers in the harvest (Matt. 9:37; Luke 10:2)

In addition, the Bible instructs us to pray for:

- ourselves (Gen. 24:12; Matt. 14:30; Luke 23:42)
- each other (James 5:16; Rom. 1:9)
- our pastors or spiritual leaders (Eph. 6:19–20; Col. 4:3)
- believers who are ill (James 5:14–15)
- government officials (1 Tim. 2:1–3)
- our enemies (Matt.5:44; Acts 7:59–60)
- Jerusalem's peace (Ps. 122:6)
- and all humankind (1 Tim. 2:1)

In the Psalms alone there are five different types of prayer requests:

- petitionary prayer for self (Ps. 13)
- confessional prayer for forgiveness (Ps. 51)
- intercessory prayer for others (Ps. 72)
- thanksgiving prayer for gratitude (Ps. 9)
- and adoration prayer for God (Ps. 113)

When you investigate what the New Testament writers asked for in their prayer requests, you discover they prayed for other believers and seldom for themselves (see sidebar). For example, in Philippians 1:9–11 the apostle Paul prayed for:

- love to abound in knowledge and judgement
- approval of things that were excellent
- sincerity without offense until the day of Christ
- fullness with the fruit of righteousness

In 2 Thessalonians 1:11-12, Paul prayed that:

- God would find them worthy of the divine call
- God would fulfill all the good pleasures of God's goodness and the work of faith with power
- the name of Jesus Christ would be glorified in his readers and in himself

Only once did Paul offer a specific prayer for himself (2 Cor. 12:8-9), and that prayer was in the midst of ministry and was no doubt intended for the furtherance of the Gospel, not the convenience of the apostle.

In the Acts of the Apostles, prayers always focused on the disciple movement, on the church, and on each other. Seldom, if ever, did one pray for self.

The prayers in the book of Revelation were likewise focused on the church—the church of that day and of the future—assuring us that prayers prayed in God's will are never lost (Rev. 8:1-4). Of the twenty-one prayers in Revelation, four come from people in this world: two by John, the author (1:5b-6; 22:20); one by the Spirit and the church; and one from the reader of the book (22:17). All the other prayers are from supernatural

Prayers of New Testament letter writers:
1 Corinthians 1:4
2 Corinthians 1:11; 13:9
Colossians 1:9–12; 2:1; 4:3
Romans 1:9–10; 15:30
Ephesians 1:15–19; 6:19–20
Philippians 1:3–11, 19
1 Thessalonians 1:2–3; 5:25
2 Thessalonians 2:13; 3:1
1 Timothy 2:1–3, 8
2 Timothy 1:3
Philemon 1:4–6, 22
Hebrews 13:18–19
3 John 1:2

beings or persons who have been translated into heaven following their death on earth:

- two by the four living creatures (4:8; 5:14)
- two by the twenty-four elders (4:11; 11:17–18)
- two by both the four living creatures and the twenty-four elders (5:9; 19:4)
- two by angels around the throne (5:12; 7:12)
- one by every created thing (5:13)
- one by souls of martyred saints (6:10)
- one by the angel of the waters (16:5-6)
- one from beside the altar (16:7)
- one by those who had conquered the beast (15:3-4)
- four by the great multitude (7:10; 19:1-3, 6-7).

While 62 percent of biblical prayers were for others, for the church, for the kingdom of God, and for the future, our prayers are generally for ourselves. Why should the focus of prayer be toward others? If the "what" of my prayer life is focused toward others and likewise other members of the family of God focus their prayers toward others, less personal burden is borne. In other words, if I know that I can share my personal prayer requests with other Christians in confidence that they will pray for me faithfully, then I do not have to carry my prayer load myself. I can be free to pray for others and for the church. The New Testament is filled with selfless prayers. So may our lives be dominated with such praying.

Prayer is found consistently in Paul's letters. Perhaps a brief look at what Paul prayed for would be helpful.

When writing to the believers in Rome, Paul prayed for unity in order that Christ might be glorified:

Now may the God who gives perseverance and encouragement grant you to be of the same mind with one another according to Christ Jesus, so that with one accord you may with one voice glorify the God and Father of our Lord Jesus Christ. (Rom. 15:5-6)

Surely the believers in Rome were as diverse as some of today's prayer groups: affluent and poor; self-educated with no formal education; conservative and liberal; multi-racial; rural and urban; old and young; gifted and common. Yet in the midst of diversity, we find our unity by looking, not at each other, but at Jesus. The glory is in his ability to make us one, not in our diversity.

A few verses later, Paul again offers a prayer for those Roman believers, this time for hope:

> Now may the God of hope fill you with all joy and peace in believing, so that you will abound in hope by the power of the Holy Spirit. (Rom. 15:13)

Here is a request for input and outflow, for filling and spilling. As the God of hope fills us, we are to be channels not reservoirs. We are to allow God's joy and peace to flow through us with hope and in the power of the Holy Spirit.

To the church in Ephesus, Paul wrote, praying for wisdom:

> That the God of our Lord Jesus Christ, the Father of glory, may give to you a spirit of wisdom and of revelation in the knowledge of Him. I pray that the eyes of your heart may be enlightened, so that you will know what is the hope of His calling, what are the riches of the glory of His inheritance in the saints, and what is the surpassing greatness of His power toward us who believe. (Eph. 1:17-19a)

As in Ephesus, so today there is much ignorance concerning the riches of God and our inheritance from God. We need not only to ask God to reveal this to us, but search God's Word in study and God's heart in prayer to discover these riches for ourselves.

To the church in Philippi, Paul wrote, praying for love:

> And this I pray, that your love may abound still more and more in real knowledge and all discernment, so that you may approve the things that are excellent, in order to be sincere and blameless until the day of Christ; having been filled with the fruit of righteousness which comes through Jesus Christ, to the glory and praise of God. (Phil. 1:9-11)

If we could just love each other as God loves us, what a difference we'd see in ourselves, our friends, and God. Our lives would exemplify discernment rather than snap judgments, excellence rather than mediocrity, sincerity rather than hypocrisy, righteousness rather than worldliness. Such love draws others through us to Christ.

To the church in Thessalonica, Paul wrote, praying for purity:

> Now may the God of peace Himself sanctify you entirely; and may your spirit and soul and body be preserved complete, without blame at the coming of our Lord Jesus Christ. (1 Thess. 5:23)

When we allow God to sanctify us, we become pure in spirit, soul, and body and devoted to being found without fault at life's end. For the church, Paul prayed for unity, hope, wisdom, love, and purity. Wherever we find Paul praying, we find believers maturing and churches growing. But what should be the wording of our prayers?

There is no pre-set, biblical pattern. The Lord's Prayer and others are models, not examples to mimic. We are to learn from them but not duplicate them. Since prayer is two-way communication, our prayer should not be pre-worded like some fill-in-the-blank generic card sent home from summer camp. As a rule, prayer should be a creative outpouring of thought formulated to communicate our ideas and concerns to God through words understood by both us and God. The Bible instructs us that prayer should be:

- humble (Luke 18: 13–14)
- confident (1 John 5:14–15)
- believing (Heb. 11:6)
- truthful (Ps. 145:18)
- persistent (Luke 18:7)
- definite (Ps. 27:4; Acts 12:5), and
- in keeping with God's will (1 John 5:14)

Is there any criteria as to how long we should pray? The Bible speaks of praying:

- all day (Ps. 25:5)
- all night (Gen. 32:24; 1 Sam. 15:10-11; 2 Sam. 12:16; Joel 1:13; Luke 6:12)
- until evening (Josh. 7:6; Judg. 20:23,26; Judg. 21:2)
- on certain days (Neh. 1:4)
- for seven days (2 Sam. 12:15-20)
- for three weeks (Dan. 10:2)
- for forty days (Deut. 9:18, 25), and

While there is no specific time limit on prayer in the Bible, there is certainly a wide range in Christian biography and thought. G. Campbell Morgan speaks of brief prayer:

> Five minutes with him in which the soul is touched by the forces of eternity will mean a day full of spiritual vigor. God can do much in five minutes of a man's time if no more can honestly be spared. He can do nothing in five minutes who should give him sixty, but who is slothful.[1]

To the other extreme, Fanny Crosby writes of "the pure delight of a single hour that before Thy throne I spend, when I kneel in prayer, and with Thee, my God, I commune as friend with friend." Since we spend approximately $1^1/_2$ to 3 hours a day eating for the nourishment of our physical bodies, should we not spend equal time on spiritual nourishment?

We are impatient people; therefore time becomes a major factor in our prayer lives. However, the more completely you can cease to be concerned about the amount of time it will take for your prayers to be answered, the more freedom you will enjoy in praying.

Now that we have considered the *who* and *what* questions, let's move on to the *where* question.

9. The Where Question:
Does Location Matter?

Location is important in life. When life began for me, I was in a particular locale. My conversion experience took place at a certain place. I have lived in several cities and likewise worked in several offices. When I die my earthly body will be "laid to rest" in a specific cemetery while my heavenly dimension will go to still another place. Location is also important to prayer, for it often determines the intensity of our prayer burden.

The stand-off and eventual storming of the Branch Davidian Complex near Waco, Texas, in the spring of 1993, resulted in the loss of many lives and affected many more. The interest level and resulting prayer burden was extremely high near the geographical location. My parents lived approximately thirty miles away and relived each day's activity on the nightly news. My wife was at our home less than a hundred miles from the Mt. Carmel complex, and likewise was a faithful news watcher. However, I was spending a portion of my Sabbatic leave teaching in the Canadian Southern Baptist Seminary in Cochrane, Alberta, Canada. Thousands of miles away, the Canadian news media gave only brief coverage to the story. My interest level was much lower than that of my family's. Yet every time I called home, it seemed all they wanted to discuss was the Branch Davidian news. Because of nearness to the location, their interest was high and their corresponding prayer burden was heavy. Because of miles, my interest and burden was less. *Where* is an important factor in praying.

Christians should pray in specific, private places. Robert Browning wrote, "God has a few men to whom he whispers." Surely, if God were to speak to you in this "still, small voice," it would be in the privacy of your prayer life. The best private place I ever had was on the back deck of our former home in Norcross, Georgia. It was my habit to arise early and see that the children were fed and that they met the school bus on time. Once the children were off to school, I would take my Bible, my notebook, and my pen, and go out on the deck overlooking our acre of pines and hardwoods. As I listened to the sounds of the trickling stream blending with the music of the birds, I would spend some time alone with God. This was not a "holy place," but it became holy because I communed with God there early in the morning.

My ministry has always been with people. Because most of us live in a climate of concern, my job is often demanding. I've found the best way to minister in the midst of people is to spend some time alone with God. Perhaps this was the discovery made also by S. D. Gordon when he wrote, "One must get alone to find out that he never is alone. The more alone we are as far as men are concerned, the least alone we are so far as God is concerned."[1]

Praying in a private place has biblical precedent:

- Abraham had a special place where he communed with God (Gen. 19:27)
- Isaac prayed in a field (Gen. 24:63)
- Daniel prayed in his private room (Dan. 6:10)
- Habakkuk prayed in his tower (Hab. 2:1)
- Jesus prayed in a "certain place" (Luke 11:1) and in the wilderness (Luke 5:16)

Jesus also taught his disciples to pray in their "inner room," or private place (Matt. 6:5-6). God has often taken servants to some out-of-the-way places for the purpose of prayer. It is occasionally on the backside of a desert—lonely, desolate, barren, uninviting, quiet, secluded—where a bush burns and a divine voice is heard.

The prayer room of John Wesley is described as follows:

> I found nothing more moving in John Wesley's house in City Road, London, than his prayer room. There is his praying chair at which he could kneel and read his Bible and lift up his heart in prayer. Standing there, I found that it took little imagination to see at prayer that smallish, upright form of one of the noblest evangelistic preachers of all time. It was, as is well-known, early in the morning that John Wesley spent most of his time at prayer. Rising at five o'clock or earlier, the day began consciously at prayer, with intercession for the saving of the people.[2]

I know a couple who decided to remodel a middle bedroom of their home into a prayer room. With all their children grown and gone, the room was available and thus put to spiritual use. I have another friend who travels much. He carries with him a small prayer rug. Whether visiting in another's home, in a hotel room, or at a conference center, he has his "place" of prayer. The small kneeling prayer bench in my office is my "where," a specific place of prayer.

Not only are Christians to practice praying in a private place, we are to pray in public places. Jesus prayed in the presence of his disciples before the last supper (Matt. 26:26; Mark 14:22; Luke 22:17; 1 Cor. 11:23-24). Likewise, Jesus prayed before the raising of Lazarus in the vicinity of the crowd of people that had gathered around that tomb (John 11:41), and in a still larger crowd Jesus prayed where the multitude needed to be fed (Mark 8:6). The Apostle Paul prayed before eating a meal (Acts 27:35) and in public worship (Acts 4:31).

There is no public place where it is inappropriate to pray. Nonbelievers feel free to call out God's name in all kinds of public places. If they can call on God's name, often in profane ways, we can call on God's name in prayerful ways. However, we should practice sensitivity. Even though he was free to pray it, some questions might be raised as to the appropriateness of the following prayer by Pastor Joe Wright of the Wichita, Kansas, Central Church, at the Kansas State Legislature:

> Heavenly Father, we come before you today to ask Your forgiveness and to seek Your direction and guidance.
>
> We know Your word says, "Woe to those who call evil good," but that is exactly what we have done. We have lost our spiritual equilibrium and inverted our values.
>
> We confess that we have ridiculed the absolute truth of Your word in the name of moral pluralism.
>
> We have worshiped other gods and called it "multiculturalism."
>
> We have endorsed perversion and called it an "alternative lifestyle."
>
> We have exploited the poor and called it "a lottery."
>
> We have neglected the needy and called it "self-preservation."
>
> We have rewarded laziness and called it "welfare."
>
> In the name of "choice," we have killed our unborn.
>
> We have neglected to discipline our children and called it "building esteem."
>
> We have abused power and called it "political savvy."
>
> We've coveted our neighbors' possessions and called it "taxes."
>
> We've polluted the air with profanity and pornography and called it "freedom of expression."
>
> We've ridiculed the time-honored values of our forefathers and called it "enlightenment."
>
> Search us, oh God, and know our hearts today. Try us, and show us any wicked way in us. Cleanse us from every sin, and set us free.
>
> Guide and bless these men and women who have been sent here by the people of Kansas and who have been ordained by You to govern this great state.
>
> Grant them Your wisdom to rule, and may their decisions direct us to the center of Your will.
>
> I ask it in the name of your son, the living savior, Jesus Christ. Amen.[3]

Paul's statement, "Therefore I want the men in every place to pray" (1 Tim. 2:8), seems to indicate that Christians are to pray not only in the private place and in the public place, but in "every place." Unless we can find some location where God doesn't exist, or where the communication between heaven and earth is out of order, there is no place that is off limits to prayer. Further, unless we find a place where we do not want God, nor need God, there is no place that is out of bounds for prayer. The location of our concern, given some appropriate sensitivity, is the location of our prayer.

Where do we find examples of prayer in the Bible? Both the Old and New Testament are filled with recorded prayers.

Here are some of the prayers which fill the Old Testament:

- Prayers for an offspring were offered by Abraham (Gen. 14:2-3), by Isaac (Gen. 25:21-23), and by Hannah (1 Sam. 1:9-13)
- Prayers for the city were offered by Abraham for Sodom (Gen. 18:23-33), by Hezekiah for Jerusalem (2 Kings 19:14-19), and by the people for Nineveh (Jon. 3).
- On an occasion a servant of Abraham prayed for a bride for Isaac (Gen. 24:12-14).
- Prayers for deliverance from danger were offered by Jacob (Gen. 32:9-12), by David (Pss. 31, 57, 142), and by sailors (Jon. 1:14).
- Moses prayed for plagues on the Egyptians (Exod. 8-12) and for the waters to part (Exod. 14:21).
- Joshua prayed for the Jordan River to part (Josh. 4:15-18).
- Moses prayed for a glimpse of the glory of God (Exod. 33:18), for a new leader (Num. 27:15-17), for a visit to Canaan (Deut. 3:23-25), and for Aaron after the making of a golden calf (Deut. 9:20).
- Joshua prayed for an extended time of daylight (Josh. 10:12).
- Gideon prayed for a sign (Judg. 16:28-31).
- Numerous prayers for forgiveness were offered by David as in his numbering the people (2 Sam. 24:10) and for his adultery with Bathsheba (Pss. 32, 51).
- Forgiveness was also requested by Manasseh (2 Chron. 33:11-13) and by Job (Job 40:3-4; 42:6).
- Solomon prayed for wisdom (2 Chron. 1:10).
- Elijah and Joel prayed for rain (1 Kings 18:42-43; Joel 1:19-20).
- David and Elijah prayed for fire (1 Chron. 21-26 and 1 Kings 18:36-37).
- Elisha prayed for spiritual vision for his servant (2 Kings 6:17).

- Hezekiah prayed for a long life (2 Kings 20:1-3).
- Jabez prayed for prosperity in his work (1 Chron. 4:10).
- Job prayed for his false friends (Job 42:7-10).
- David prayed for guidance in war (1 Sam. 17:45; 30:8; 2 Sam 2:1, 5:19).
- Daniel and his friends prayed for the interpretation of a dream (Dan. 2:18).
- Prayers for healing were offered by Abraham for Abimelech (Gen. 20:17-18), by David for his ill child (2 Sam. 12:16), and by a godly man for Jeroboam (1 Kings 13:6).
- Elijah and Elisha prayed for resurrection (1 Kings 17:20-21; 2 Kings 4:33-35).
- The welfare of Israel was the theme of several prayers: Jacob's (Gen. 48-49), Israel's (Exod. 2:23), Moses' (Exod. 32:31-32; Num. 10:35-36; 11:1-2; 21:7-9), and Israel's (Judg. 1:1).
- The forgiveness of Israel was prayed for by Israel (Judg. 10:10), Moses (Num. 14:13-19), David (Ps. 85), Jeremiah (Jer. 14:20-22), Daniel (Dan. 9), Ezra (Ezra 9:5; 10:4), Nehemiah (Neh. 1:4-11), and Habakkuk (Hab. 3).
- Prayer was offered for the sanctification of Israel's temple (1 Kings 8:22-54).

The New Testament is likewise filled with prayers:

- Zacharias prayed for an offspring (Luke 1:13).
- Prayers for deliverance from danger were offered by the disciples (Matt. 8:24-25), by Peter (Matt. 14:28-31), and by the members of the Jerusalem church (Acts 12:5).
- The disciples prayed for someone to replace Judas (Acts 1:24-25).
- Forgiveness was requested by the prodigal son (Luke 15:17-19).
- A rich man prayed for relief from Hell (Luke 16:22-31).
- The disciples prayed for boldness in proclaiming their faith (Acts 4:24-30).
- Stephen prayed for those who were killing him (Acts 7:59-60).
- The ministry of the Holy Spirit was prayed for by the disciples (Acts 8:14-15), by Peter (Acts 11:5) and by Paul (Acts 19:6).

- Paul prayed at his conversion (Acts 9:5-6), for a successful missionary journey (Rom. 1:9-11), for the salvation of Israel (Rom. 10:1), for the removal of his "thorn in the flesh" (2 Cor. 12:7-10), and for Timothy's successful ministry (2 Tim. 1:3-6)
- Paul prayed for the welfare of the church in Rome (Rom. 1:8-10), in Ephesus (Eph. 1:15-16, 3:13-21), in Philippi (Phil. 1:2-7), in Colosse (Col. 1:1-14), and in Thessalonica (1 Thess. 1:2-3; 3:9-13; 2 Thess. 1:3, 11-12; 2:13, 16-17).
- Paul prayed for specific issues among the believers in Rome (Rom. 15:5-6, 13), Ephesus (Eph. 1:17-19a), Philippi (Phil. 1:9-11), and Thessalonica (1 Thess. 5:23).
- The church members in Antioch prayed for Paul and Silas (Acts 13:3).
- Prayers for their own healing were offered by: a leper (Matt. 8:2), a man in chains (Mark 5:6), an ill woman (Matt. 9:20-21), two blind men (Matt. 9:27), Bartimaeus (Mark 10:46-47), a deaf and dumb man (Mark 7:32-34), and ten lepers (Luke 17:12-16).
- Prayers for the healing of others were offered by: a centurion for his servant (Matt. 8:5-9), Jairus for his daughter (Matt. 9:18), a Canaanite mother for her daughter (Matt. 15:21-28), a father for his son (Matt. 17:14-16), an official for his son (John 4:46-50), Mary and Martha for Lazarus (John 11:30), and by Paul for the father-in-law of Publius (Acts 28:8),
- Peter prayed for resurrection (Acts 9:36-43).
- Prayer was offered for Jerusalem (Heb. 13:20-21).
- Peter prayed for Pontus, Galatia, Cappadocia, Asia, and Bithynia (1 Pet. 5:10- 11).

Among the prayers in the book of Revelation, the martyred saints prayed for justice (Rev. 6:10). Those who had been slain for their testimony cried out, "How long, O Lord, holy and true, wilt Thou refrain from judging and avenging our blood on those who dwell on the earth?" (Rev. 6:10). Jesus had predicted many would die for their faith (Matt. 24:9). Now these cry out with an echo from the Old Testament (Ps. 6:3, 13:1-2, 35:17, 59:5, 79:5-10, 80:4, 89:46, 90:13, 94:3; Isa. 6:11; Jer. 47:6; Zech. 1:12; Hab. 1:2).

Professor Robert E. Coleman said of this type of prayer:

> It is a good question—one that honest hearts have been asking through centuries, especially in times of adversity. That the query is heard in heaven certainly absolves it from any sinful propensity. This is a natural cry of human nature in prolonged waiting, which in this setting rises to the very throne of the Most High, intoned with praises of His sovereignty.1 The final prayer of the Bible is in Revelation 22:20–21. Here the aged apostle John, looking across the sea from Patmos toward those he loved and would likely not see again until Heaven, prays to the coming King, "Come, Lord, Jesus" (Rev. 22:20). Then this final benediction is offered, "The grace of the Lord Jesus be with all. Amen" (Rev. 22:21).[4]

The final prayer of the Bible is in Revelation 22:20–21. Here the aged apostle John, looking across the sea from Patmos toward those he loved and would likely not see again until heaven, prays to the coming King, "Come, Lord Jesus" (Rev. 22:20). Then this final benediction is offered: "The grace of the Lord Jesus be with all. Amen" (Rev. 22:21).

From Genesis to Revelation the Bible is filled with prayers. In his book *All the Prayers of the Bible*, Herbert Lockyer says, "Exclusive of the Psalms, which form a prayer-book on their own, the Bible records no fewer than 650 definite prayers, of which no less than 450 have recorded answers."[5]

We're halfway through the questions of the prayer-shaped disciple. From *who*, *what*, and *where*, we go to the *when* question.

10. The When Question:
It's All in the Timing

"When will we get there?" "When do we eat?" "When are we going to open Christmas presents?" "When will I be old enough to drive?" These and others are questions children ask their earthly fathers. There are similar *when* questions that we ask our heavenly Father.

Often our response to the news of an event is "when did it happen?" or "when will it be over?" Once we know "when," we determine our response. Depending on when, our concern lessens or intensifies, our stress level rises or falls, our plans remain the same or change.

Two weeks before my departure for West Africa to speak to the missionaries in Gambia and Burkina Faso at their annual spiritual retreat, I was seated in the bleachers at the eighteenth green of the Colonial Golf Tournament. It was a beautiful spring day for golf, no clouds overhead, a gentle breeze, temperature in the upper eighties, and bright sunshine. When I jumped off the side of the bleachers to move to another location for a better viewing, my foot caught, sending me to the pavement below, head first. I landed on my right side. An ambulance ride and two hours in the emergency room later, I was told I had a dislocated and fractured right shoulder, a partially torn rotator cuff, and a deep bruise on my right elbow. Later, nerve damage was discovered in my right arm. The timing couldn't have been worse. For the first week following the accident, it appeared I wouldn't get to go to West Africa and my prayer intensified. I posed the "when" question often. "When" would I be well? "When" would the doctor release me? Finally he reluctantly agreed to let me go if I would take it easy. The "when" question had subsided temporarily.

While we should pray at all times, the Christian should also pray at specific times. The tradition of Jews which involved praying twice a day (the hours of sacrifice, at sunrise and sunset, or the third and ninth hours) is very old (Ezra 9:5; Dan. 9:21). There is also the old tradition of prayer at midday (the sixth hour), establishing three times of prayer (Ps. 55:17; Dan. 6:10). In addition there was the established tradition of giving thanks to God before a meal (Deut. 8:10; Mark 6:41; Rom. 14:6; 1 Cor. 10:30; 1 Tim. 4:4), which the Christian church adopted later. On yet another occasion, the psalmist said he prayed in the day and the night (Ps. 88:1). The psalmist joined Isaiah in announcing that he prayed to the Lord every morning (Isa. 33:2; Pss. 5:3; 88:13; 143:8).

It was the pattern of Jesus to pray "in the early morning, while it was still dark" (Mark 1:35). It is said that during the great Methodist revivals a secret to early morning prayer was learned: go to bed by 9:00 P.M. In our own rushed society, prayer may well depend on rising early. If the beginning of the day slips by without prayer, the busy agenda of the rest of the day makes it difficult to recapture a lost meeting time with God.

On the other hand, the danger of the early morning prayer time is captured by John Baille: "Yet let me not, when this morning prayer is said, think my worship ended and spend the day in forgetfulness of Thee."[1] Nevertheless, the historical pattern has followed the early morning model of Jesus. John Wesley spent two hours daily in prayer beginning at four in the morning, and Martin Luther said, "If I fail to spend two hours in prayer each morning, the devil gets the victory through the day. I have so much business I cannot get on without spending three hours daily in prayer."[2] When all is said and done, we usually work our prayer times around our personal schedule. Jesus, on the other hand, worked his schedule around his prayer life.

On one occasion Jesus prayed all night (Luke 6:12). In fact, if you could have seen him "coming forth in the morning to preach the Gospel and heal the sick, you might have seen how his garments were covered with the dew that had fallen upon him as he had knelt all night in prayer to his father."[3] There seemed to be in the life of our Lord specific times when he prayed and these dictated the remainder of his schedule.

The pattern of the early church related to prayer is expressed in the Acts of the Apostles. It is said that Peter and John prayed in the middle of the afternoon which was the ninth hour or approximately 3:00 P.M. (Acts 3:1), and that Peter prayed at noon, the sixth hour (Acts 10:9). Christians should pray at specific times, for there is no substitute for the divine appointment when we close out the world and commune with God alone. This is in stark contrast to the non-specific, non-appointed time for prayer. While "fervency is an appropriate form of active prayer, frenzy is not."[4] If we would incorporate into our lifestyle the pattern of praying at specific, appointed times, no situation would find us unprepared for the practice of praying.

In between our set times of prayer or in addition to our set prayer agendas, we may feel burdened to pray for someone or some event. Those in need may be depending on our sensitivity to God's prayer-timing. Such was the case with Southern Baptist missionaries Bill and Sharon Gilbert. Acting on faith that friends and family in the U.S. were interceding for their safety, the Gilberts escaped from Iraqi-controlled Kuwait during the Gulf War. Their escape was in a bullet-pierced, church-owned car across forty-five miles of desert and through a line of Iraqi tanks. Upon reaching the Saudi Arabian border, Bill Gilbert said, "We left Monday morning about five o'clock and made the two-hour trek to the border." Linda added that they timed their escape for sunrise Monday because she felt certain their friends in the United States would be praying for them during Sunday evening worship services. What if friends had been in a business-as-usual mode and not been sensitive to the timing of the Gilberts' need? Timing is crucial.

Not only should Christians pray at specific times and at burdened times, but the Bible teaches that we should pray at all times. Jesus said, "Keep on the alert at all times, praying in order that you may have strength to escape all these things that are about to take place" (Luke 21:36). On yet another occasion Jesus told "a parable to show that at all times they ought to pray" (Luke 18:1). The early church is described as, "These all with one mind were continually devoting themselves to prayer" (Acts 1:14). Paul wrote, "With all prayer and petition pray at all times" (Eph. 6:18) and further instructed believers to "pray without ceasing" (1 Thess. 5:17).

What does it mean to pray continually? Perhaps it might be likened to the way airline personnel stay in touch with the control tower. On a flight from Los Angeles to Hawaii, we were allowed headphones to listen to communication between the cockpit crew and the tower. It was interesting to note, as we moved from one control base station to another across the Pacific Ocean, the communications officer did not talk to the station at all times, nor did the control personnel talk to the communications officer at all times, but at all times communication was possible.

This idea of praying continually might be further illustrated by the pager attached to one's belt. Those who wear these do not communicate all the time, but they are reachable at all times. Lloyd John Ogilvie found it helpful to think of praying without ceasing like breathing: "All through the day I try to remember to breathe out the prayer, 'Lord, I need You!' and breath in with the prayer of receptive attitude, 'Lord, I receive you!'"[5]

The necessity of continual communication with God through prayer is illustrated further by the number of hours per week spent in specific praying. There are 168 hours in a week. Let's assume you sleep eight hours per night. That reduces your potential time spent in conscious prayer by fifty-six hours leaving you only 112 hours per week to spend specifically praying. Let's assume further that you pray fifteen minutes in the morning and fifteen minutes at night at specific times. This thirty minutes of specific praying per day times seven days means that you pray 3 ½ hours per week at set times. That leaves 108 ½ hours per week of no prayer, unless, of course, you pray "without ceasing."

Some have suggested using visual aids to remind us to pray continually. When you see a hospital sign, you could be reminded to pray for those who offer professional health care. A school zone sign could serve as a reminder to pray for students and educators. A state or national flag could serve as a reminder to pray for those in places of governmental authority. Any vision of food stores, advertisements, or food itself could remind you to be thankful for "daily bread." Caution lights could call you to ask God for patience and discernment. The list is endless.

In the time between the ascension of Jesus and the Day of Pentecost, the disciples were "continually devoting themselves to prayer, along with the women, and Mary the mother of Jesus, and with His brothers" (Acts 1:14). This is one of our prayer models. Surely if we are praying "without ceasing," no time will catch us off guard.

Shortly after moving to Fort Worth, Texas, I received a brochure in the mail informing me of the newly installed 911 Emergency Telephone System in our city. Among other features, the brochure said, I could dial 911 on my telephone at any time and get an immediate response. Even if I could not utter a word into the phone, help would still be on the way. Fantastic, but not entirely new. When I accepted Jesus Christ as my personal Savior and Lord, a similar emergency system was activated in my life. I can call on the Lord at any time and receive a response. Even if my circumstances do not allow time for a spoken prayer, still help is on the way. God said, "Before they call, I will answer; and while they are still speaking, I will hear" (Isa. 65:24). Karl Barth said it this way: "It may well be that he can only sigh, stammer and mutter. But so long as it is a request brought before God, God will hear it and understand it."[6]

What an assurance to know I can call upon the Lord at all times and receive a response. Concerning this constant prayer, John Killinger remarked:

It is no wonder that there was an outpouring of spirit at Pentecost, and that such tremendous crowds responded to the preaching of Simon Peter. I have said to my preaching students that if they could get only five persons in their churches to pray like that, they would have little Pentecosts every time they come together.[7]

The prayer-shaped disciple prays through the *who, what, where,* and *when* questions. We have explored these and now it is time for the *why* question.

11. The Why Question:
A Child's Adult Question

The most frequently asked question, especially by children, is "Why?" God, who gave us inquisitive minds, must surely have anticipated our *why* questions.

I was in the midst of speaking to a group of missionaries on the need for having people praying for them as they went about their missionary tasks, when one raised his hand and asked, "God has indeed called me to this place, so why do I need people praying for me? Is not the God who placed me here, more than able to protect and enable me here, with or without the prayers of others?" The *why* question had surfaced again.

Why should a Christian pray? A Christian should pray because the Bible teaches prayer. From Adam and Eve communicating with God in the Garden of Eden (Gen. 3:1-19), the first specific reference to prayer in Genesis 4:26, and the first use of the word "pray" in Genesis 20:7 to the last mention of the word "prayers" in Revelation 8:4 and John's final prayer on the island of Patmos (Rev. 22:20), the Bible teaches prayer. Jacob prayed when he encountered an angel. Solomon prayed while he ministered in the Temple. The psalmist prayed both in preparation for and in the midst of his psalms. The Israelites prayed throughout their time of captivity. Moses prayed on Mt. Sinai and elsewhere. Job prayed in the midst of persecution and frustration. The prophets prayed in their expectation of the promised Messiah. Jesus prayed alone and in the midst of crowds. The Apostle Paul prayed all over the Mediterranean world. From the early days of Adam's communication with God to the later days of John's vision of the eternal, the Bible teaches prayer. The Bible teaches prayer so:

- we might "delight" God (Prov. 15:8). All that God does is for God's glory. We pray because God allows us to pray, but in so doing, we delight God, and thus God receives glory;
- we will not "lose heart" (Luke 18:1);
- "the Father may be glorified in the Son" (John 14:13);
- we might be "strengthened with power through His Spirit in the inner man" (Eph. 3:16);
- we "may be healed" (James 5:16);
- we might increase our "wisdom" (James 1:5);
- the "peace of God" (Phil. 4:7) will guard our hearts and minds;
- we will "find compassion" (Prov. 28:13);
- we may "make known with boldness the mystery of the gospel" (Eph. 6:19).

Likewise, the Christian should pray because Jesus Christ modeled prayer. In the Gospels there are twenty-four references to Jesus praying. Of all the verbs used to describe what Jesus did—tell, ask, follow, go, abide, do—none is used more than "pray." The first glimpse of Jesus after the accounts of his birth find him in the Temple, which he called the "house of prayer." In studying the context of Jesus' prayers, we gain insight into why we should pray (see sidebar).

Further, Jesus warned his followers to avoid praying with the pride of the Pharisee who "prayed about himself" (Luke 18:11 NIV) and to avoid the ignorance of the pagan who prayed with "meaningless repetition" (Matt. 6:7).

Finally, Christians should pray because our lives require a prayer relationship with God. Of major importance to an understanding of the biblical concept of prayer is a realization that we were created to respond to God.

Prayers Jesus prayed:

1. Luke 3:21, at his baptism.
2. Mark 1:35, early in the morning following a busy day.
3. Luke 5:16, amid pressing duties.
4. Luke 6:12 ,all night before calling out the twelve.
5. Mark 6:41; Matt. 14:19; Luke 9:16; John 6:11, at the feeding of the five thousand.
6. Mark 6:46–48; John 6:15; Matt. 14:23, after feeding the five thousand, when the multitude wanted to make him king.
7. Mark 8:6–7; Matt. 15:36, at the feeding of the four thousand.
8. Luke 9:18, before the question, "Who do men say I am?"
9. Luke 9:28, on the mount of transfiguration.
10. Luke 10:21; Matt. 11:25–26, upon the return of the seventy.
11. Luke 11:1, in the presence of his disciples, leading them to request, "Lord, teach us to pray."
12. John 11:41– 42, at the tomb of Lazarus.
13. Matt. 19:13–15, when he blessed the children.
14. John 12:27–30, at the coming of the Greeks.
15. Luke 22:32, at the intercession for Peter.
16. Mark 14:22–23; Matt. 26:26–27; Luke 22:19–20; 1 Cor. 11:24–25, at the institution of the Lord's supper.
17. John 17:1–26, the great High Priestly prayer.
18. Matt. 26:36–44; Luke 22:39–46; Mark 14:32–39, in Gethsemane.
19. Luke 23:34, from the Cross: "Father, forgive them, for they know not what they do."
20. Mark 15:34; Matt. 27:46, from the Cross: "My God, my God, why hast Thou forsaken me?"
21. Luke 23:46, from the Cross: "Father, into Thy hands I commit my Spirit."
22. Luke 24:30, at the meal with the two in Emmaus.
23. Heb. 7:25; Rom. 8:34, interceding for believers.
24. Heb. 5:7, praying with tears.

The nature of our prayer relationship with God is such that it causes us to deeply desire God's presence in our life. When you love someone, you want to be in their presence. When that physical presence is impossible, you desire to communicate with that person by whatever means are available. When I am traveling, as I often am, I seldom miss a day communicating with my family. Even though my physical presence is impossible, I can telephone, fax, or e-mail, thus allowing me to stay in touch with those whom I love. It is the very nature of my relationship with my family. How much more, then, should communication be the nature of my relationship with God? When I am in touch daily with God, praying is much easier.

The purpose of our prayer relationship with God is not to get gifts, for God knows what we need before we ask. The purpose of it is to get to know God. Indeed, prayer is not reaching for things in the hand of God, nor for answers in the mind of God, but it is reaching for the very hand and mind of God. Prayer is the scale on which we balance an awareness of our need to communicate with God with an awareness of God's greater need to communicate with us.

Why would you or anyone need prayer support if God had indeed called you to a specific place and/or ministry? Would God's own powerful presence not be enough to sustain you without the intercessory prayers of God's people?

While there is much scripture related to God's providential care (see Deut. 2:7 and others), there is also clear evidence that God intends for and expects followers to pray for each other. Why else would Jesus have prayed for his called and chosen disciples in John 17? Here Jesus prayed for unity (17:11), for joy (17:13), for protection from the enemy (17:15), for sanctification and holiness (17:17), and for eternal fellowship with him (17:24). Not only did our Lord intercede for his disciples then, but now he "lives to make intercession for them" (Heb. 7:25). If we don't need intercession, why did God give Jesus the ongoing assignment to intercede for all?

Likewise, Paul, a called and committed missionary, understood his need for intercessors. He wrote to Timothy, his son in the faith and ministry, urging, "entreaties and prayers, petitions and thanksgivings, be made on behalf of all men" (1 Tim. 2:1). To the believers at Thessalonica, Paul humbly requested, "Brethren, pray for us" (1 Thess. 5:25), and to the believers in Ephesus, he begged, "pray on my behalf . . . " (Eph. 6:19). Paul, who understood his clear call to ministry, also understood his need for the intercessory prayer support of fellow believers.

Also, in the history of the advancement of Christianity, numerous examples appear of the value of intercessory prayer for those called by God to special tasks. The following account from the life of D. L. Moody illustrates this truth:

> After the Chicago fire Moody went to London to rest and to study from Bible scholars. He had no intention of preaching. But one Sunday Moody accepted an offer to preach. The service dragged on; Moody wished he had never agreed to preach.
>
> Meanwhile, a woman in London had heard of Moody's work in America and had asked God to send Moody to London. This woman was an invalid. On that particular Sunday, her sister was present at church when Moody preached. When her sister reached home she asked the woman, "Guess who spoke this morning: Mr. Moody from Chicago!" The woman turned pale, and said, "This is an answer to my prayer. If I had known that he was to preach at church, I should have eaten nothing this morning, and waited on God in prayer. Leave me alone this afternoon. Do not let anyone come to see me; do not send me anything to eat."
>
> All afternoon the woman gave herself to prayer. As Moody preached that night, he became conscious of a different atmosphere in the church. The powers of an unseen world seemed to fall upon him and his hearers. As he drew his message to a close, Moody was impressed to give an invitation. He asked those who wanted to accept Christ to rise. Four or five hundred people stood.
>
> Moody thought they misunderstood him and so put the question several ways. But the people had understood . . . The religious awakening of Great Britain came from that beginning.[1]

Yet another illustration of the power of intercessory prayer for one who is called by God comes from the life of Charles Finney:

> In Uttica, Syracuse, Binghamton, Rochester and Rome, great numbers of people were aroused to a new earnestness about sin. Many repented and committed their lives to Jesus Christ. Religion permeated society and business. It controlled ambition.

People assumed that Finney was responsible for this revival but there was another man who had part in this revival. His name was Able Clary.

Finney had known Clary since boyhood and had the greatest respect for him. Clary never appeared in public gatherings. He was an educated man who was licensed to preach; but he preached little. Instead, he was so burdened with the souls of men that he devoted hours to intercession.

Lying in bed with tuberculosis, Clary would pull up a small table and write in his journal day by day. "My heart has been moved to pray for Uttica, Syracuse, Binghamton, Rochester and Rome."

After Clary's death, Finney discovered Clary's prayer journal. Finney found in the exact order of the burden laid upon Clary's heart was the order of blessing poured upon his ministry. Among other entries, he discovered notes of Ceylon. Looking into the records of the American Mission Board, Finney noticed there was a great spiritual awakening in Ceylon at the time Clary was impressed to pray."[2]

While God's presence and power are adequate for those whom God calls to special assignments, they would be well advised to diligently seek the intercessory prayer support of fellow believers.

We have just one question left to consider. From *who, what, where, when*, and *why*, we move finally to *how*. Then we will have considered the prayer-shaped disciple praying through the six communication questions.

12. The How Question:
When All Else Fails, Read the Instructions

Before coffee break on the morning of April 19, 1995, a rental truck full of explosives blew-up in front of the Alfred P. Murrah Federal Building in downtown Oklahoma City, creating massive destruction of life and property and giving the world a series of *how* questions related to praying. Within hours, I received phone calls from two newspaper reporters who were writing articles on prayer in a time of crisis. They both asked the same question, "How does one pray in times like these?" Thus, the final of the six communication questions to be considered is the *how* question.

One of the *how* question relates to how crisis praying differs from non-crisis praying. Many believers get serious about prayer only at these times. Suffice it to say that praying in times of crisis will be much more effective if the person praying has an ongoing discipline of regular prayer. Crisis praying by its nature is a spasmodic cry of emergency rather than the habitual communication of a godly life. If you are accustomed to walking and talking with God consistently, you would not want to drift so far that you would have to call loudly in the time of crisis. In other words, our ability to pray when not in crisis measures our ability to pray effectively when in crisis.

Nevertheless, Jesus modeled for us how to pray at these times. In the Garden of Gethsemane, Jesus taught us to first face the crisis head-on in prayer: "Sit here while I go over there and pray" (Matt. 26:36). Second, Jesus defined the crisis, "My soul is deeply grieved, to the point of death" (Matt. 26:38). Third, Jesus evaluated the options: "My Father, if it is possible, let this cup pass from Me" (Matt. 26:39). Finally, our Lord came to a firm decision, "My Father . . . Your will be done" (Matt. 26:42). In Luke's account of the Gethsemane experience, another dimension of crisis praying appears, namely that Jesus was empowered to face the crisis: "An angel from heaven appeared to Him, strengthening Him" (Luke 22:43).

There are other *how* questions. How should we address God? The answer ranges from Abba to awesome. On one extreme, we should address God as though we were talking to our loving father, our Abba. This includes respect, but it also includes acquaintance. It is distant, yet personal (Matt. 26:42; Rom. 8:15; Gal. 4:6). On the other hand, we should address God as the awesome, majestic, powerful God of all creation. Addressing God in prayer ranges from "Father, We Adore You" to "Holy, Holy, Holy, Lord God Almighty"; from "Daddy's Hands" to "A Mighty Fortress is Our God"; from "What a Friend We Have in Jesus" to "What a Mighty God We Serve." Don't stay on either extreme for long. Balance the personality of God with the prayer address of the believer. As D. L. Moody said, "We are to ask with a beggar's humility, to seek with a servant's carefulness, and to knock with the confidence of a friend."[1]

How should we posture ourselves before God in prayer? Bodily posture in praying varies (see sidebar). In the final analysis, bodily posture is irrelevant when there is an urgent need for prayer. As Sam Walter Foss reminds us in his poem "Myriad Ways," any posture in prayer is appropriate if it works:

> "The proper way for a man to pray,"
> Said Deacon Lemuel Keyes,
> "And the only proper attitude
> Is down upon his knees."

Some biblical postures for prayer:

Falling down prostrate before God:
Genesis 17:3
Numbers 16:22; 20:6
Ezekiel 1:28; 3:23; 9:8; 11:13; 43:3; 44:4
Matthew 4:9; 26:39

Standing:
Genesis 24:12–14
Exodus 33:10
1 Kings 8:14, 22, 55
2 Kings 23:3
2 Chronicles20:9,13,19
Nehemiah 9:4–5
Matthew 6:5
Mark 11:25
Luke 18:13

Standing with hands outstretched:
Genesis 48:14–15
1 Kings 8:54
2 Chronicles 6:13
Ezra 9:5–6
Job 11:13–15
Psalms 88:9; 143:6
Isaiah 1:15

Seated:
Judges 20:26
2 Samuel 7:18
1 Kings 19:4
1 Chronicles17:16
Nehemiah 1:4

Laying in bed:
Psalms 4:4; 63:3

With laying on of hands:
Acts 6:6; 13:3; 28:8

Kneeling:
1 Kings 8:54; 19:18
2 Kings 1:13
2 Chronicles 6:13
Ezra 9:5
Psalm 95:6
Daniel 6:10
Matt. 17:14–15
Mark 1:40; 10:17
Luke 5:8; 22:41
Acts 20:36; 21:4–5
Ephesians 3:14–16

With hands lifted up:
Genesis 48:14–15
Exodus 17:11–14
1 Kings 8:54
2 Chronicles6:13
Ezra 9:5–6
Psalms 28:2; 88:9; 141:2
Lamentations 3:41
1 Timothy 2:8

With head bowed:
Exodus 4:31; 12:27

With eyes lifted toward heaven:
Genesis 14:22
Nehemiah 8:6
Psalms 28:2; 63:4; 123:1–2
Lamentations 2:19
John 11:41; 17:1
1 Timothy 2:8

While walking (implied):
Joshua 6:1–20
Numbers 13:1–33
Luke 10:1–3

"No, I should say the way to pray,"
    Said the Reverend Doctor Wise,
"Is standing straight with outstretched arms,
    And rapt and upturned eyes."

"On, no, no, no," said Elder Snow,
    "Such posture is too proud;
A man should pray with eyes fast closed,
    And head contritely bowed."
"It seems to me his hands should be
    Austerely clasped in front,
With both thumbs pointed toward the ground,"
    Said Reverend Doctor Blunt.

"Last year I fell in Hidgin's well
    Head first," said Cyrus Brown.
"With both my heels a stickin' up,
    My head a-pointin' down;
An' I made a prayer right then an' there—
    Best prayer I ever said,
The prayingest prayer I ever prayed,
    Was a-standing on my head!"

Another important question is how do we hear from God? Teresa of Ávila, a Spanish writer on religion, says, "We ought to address ourselves to prayer rather in order to listen than to speak." As important as hearing from God is, it is always based on God's time, never on ours. You will hear from God in the midst of doing God's will, that is "as you go." Indeed, it is a well-known axiom of the psychology of perception that we succeed in listening only as we respond in some way to what we have heard. Thus, God continues to communicate with us as we are faithful in doing what we know God wants us to do.

I asked God on one occasion to give me ideas for a seminar on prayer. With one week to go, I still didn't have any sure direction as to what I would do with the four sessions I would be teaching. One day as I left the office and drove home, I asked God again to give me inspiration. Long ago I learned to keep a legal pad with me in the car, for God often speaks to me "as I go." As I drove with one hand and wrote with the other hand, I received strange stares from fellow motorists. The point is we often hear from God "as we go."

But we also hear in the midst of waiting on God's timing or "as we wait." Like parents with children, we must wait for the benefit of the children to tell some things that we already know. So the Father waits to reveal some things to us and we hear only as we are patient in our waiting for God's communication. Bill Huebsch helps us understand how to hear from God in this manner as he writes:

> For many people, prayer is a consumer commodity. We pray for things: rain, peace, health, success. And when we get what we ask for, we believe our prayer is responsible for it. If we don't get it, we switch into another way of thinking and wonder whether we prayed wrong, or whether God just knew better . . . We think of prayer as something we do in order to get something else. It's a commodity to be traded for favors from God, who in our judgement would not bestow these favors without sufficient supplication. . . . Our role is simply to pause and allow prayer to emerge in us, naturally. It is for us to turn down the volume of our own words long enough to hear the Word of God.[2]

How is it that sometimes we do not hear from God? There are lifestyle characteristics that keep us from hearing him. Indeed, God not only hears our prayers, but hears our whole life. Therefore, God does not just respond to what you say, but responds also to what you are.

One evening I arrived at the New Orleans airport, rented a car, and headed west on Interstate 10 toward a speaking engagement. Not far ahead of me I saw flashing red lights and assumed there had been an automobile accident. However, it was a road block. The temperature had dropped to such a level that the lightly falling mist had begun to freeze on the overpasses that crossed the bayou country of south Louisiana. I had to detour around the bridges. The detours did not prevent me from arriving at my destination; they simply slowed me down and inconvenienced me on the journey. Just as there are road blocks in the human transportation system, there are "prayer blocks" in the spiritual communication system. These "prayer blocks" do not keep us from communicating with God.

Some prayer blocks that keep you from hearing God:

Failure to forgive those who have wronged you (Matt. 6:14–15).

Failure to pray in the name/within the will of Jesus (John 14:13–14).

False pride (Luke 18:10–14; Job 35:12).

Failure to abide in Christ and let his words abide in you (John 15:7).

Disobedience (Eph. 5:6; 1 Sam. 8:18; 28:4–6).

Prying for the wrong or carnal motives (James 4:3).

Praying while doubting God will respond (James 1:6–7).

Failure to keep God's commands (1 John 3:22; Deut. 1:43–45).

Allowing unconfessed sin to dwell within you (Ps. 66:18; Isa. 59:2).

Failure to maintain peace in the home (1 Pet. 3:7).

Failure to ask according to God's will (1 John 5:14).

Being a hypocrite or being insincere (Matt. 6:5).

Failure to hear the cry of the poor (Prov. 21:13).

Failure to pray earnestly (Jer. 29:13).

Failure to be serious in prayer (1 Pet. 4:7).

Failure to listen when God communicates (Zech. 7:13).

Failure to hear the law of God (Prov. 28:9).

Insincere worship (Isa. 1:12–15).

Straying from God (Jer. 14:10–12).

Neglecting the council of God (Prov. 1:24-30).

Failure to persist in prayer (Luke 11:5–10).

An unforgiving attitude (Matt. 5:23–24).

Worshiping anything (idols) in place of God (Ezek. 14:6–11; 20:31).

Refusing to be restored and/or revived (Ps. 80:3–4, 18b).

Doing evil (1 Pet. 3:12).

They simply slow communication and inconvenience the process. In short, they keep us from hearing God adequately.

Who has not put together an object whose assembly included a complicated set of instructions? To just get *through* the task we needed instructions for understanding the instructions. Prayer should be better understood and practiced now that you have thought *through* the *who*, *what*, *where*, *when*, *why*, and *how* instructions. It is time to move *beyond* in our quest to be prayer-shaped disciples.

The Prayer-Shaped Disciple Prays *Beyond*

Perhaps the greatest example of *beyond* praying began when Jeremiah Lanphier, a Presbyterian lay-missionary, called a prayer meeting at 12:00 noon on Wednesday, September 23, 1857, at the old North Dutch Reformed Church. He had no idea what the results would be. His church was in decline as members relocated further away from the church. That Wednesday, he waited in the church located at the corner of Fulton and William Streets on Manhattan Island, New York City. After a few minutes, another man arrived, then another, until six were present. They prayed and asked God for revival. The next Wednesday, there were thirteen present; the next Wednesday, twenty-four; and in the weeks following, the group continued to grow.

Eventually they began to meet daily at noon. By February of 1858, every church on Manhattan Island was filled with people praying. New York City was seeing an average of 10,000 converts per week. By March 1858, religion was the topic of discussion on the streets as most churches in New York City were filled with praying men. Horace Greeley sent a reporter around to count how many men were praying. Upon his return he apologized, saying he could only get around to twelve prayer meetings and could only count 6,100.

The prayer revival spread to Brooklyn, then down the Eastern seaboard. In Philadelphia, 6,000 people gathered daily for prayer with the result of 5,000 conversions. In New Jersey, there were reports of over 60,000 converts. At Princeton, 40 percent of the student body was saved with 18 percent committing to enter the ministry. The revival spread across the Appalachian Mountain range and down the Ohio Valley. Louisville's Masonic Hall overflowed daily with praying men. Meeting halls in Cincinnati were unable to accommodate the crowds. In Cleveland, there were 2,000 in prayer daily out of a population of 40,000.

In Kalamazoo, Michigan, the Baptists, Methodists, Presbyterians, and Congregationalists united in prayer at the YMCA. One day the leader read a note: "A praying wife requests the prayers of this meeting for her unconverted husband." Six men rose to their feet and admitted to being the unconverted husband. There were 400–500 conversions in the town. Over a period of approximately eight months 250,000 conversions were reported in America, and it all began in a prayer meeting of six men.

While in New York City recently, I went looking for the North Dutch Reformed Church, launching pad for the great prayer revivals of 1857–58. Almost as if seeking some bit of holy ground, I took the subway to Lower Manhattan, got off at the Fulton Street exit, and walked south to the intersection of Fulton and William Streets. The old North Dutch Reformed Church was gone. It had long ago been destroyed. The four corner lots were now occupied by the Aetna Life Insurance Company, a major bank, the office of the General Nutrition Company, and the subway office for New York City. It didn't take long to realize that the spot once occupied by a prayer meeting was now occupied, symbolically at least, by the very things we have turned to as substitutes for prayer. Rather than seek our strength and our sustenance from God, we have turned to securities, represented by the insurance office; investments, represented by the bank; the good life, represented by the nutrition center; and the ability to travel somewhere else to find happiness, represented by the subway office.

What happened to the North Dutch Reformed Church? What happened to prayer? We have substituted security, investments, health, and travel. The old North Dutch Reformed Church isn't there anymore. It is amazing that 140 years from the great revivals that swept America, I could not find one plaque, one cornerstone, or one memento of any kind at the location of the beginnings of those revivals. What's happened to prayer? It has not only been replaced, it has, for many, been forgotten along with the revival that it brings.

When will God's people be revived again and God's kingdom come on earth? It will be when we begin again to pray beyond the basics, beyond the private prayer closet, beyond to the church, beyond to the world, beyond into spiritual warfare.

13. Basic Ingredients:
Mighty ACTS

Earlier we looked at the four basic ingredients of prayer (Adoration, Confession, Thanksgiving, Supplication). Now we must learn to pray beyond the basic ingredients. Prayer is more than just ACTS; it's MIGHTY ACTS. God said, "Call to Me, and I will answer you, and I will tell you great and *mighty* things, which you do not know" (Jer. 33:3). So, let's expand the acronym to include six more ingredients to prayer using the word MIGHTY:

The *M* implies Meditation. The Biblical basis for meditation is ample. God said, "In quietness and trust is your strength" (Isa. 30:15). The psalmist continually makes reference to meditating (see list). The only place in the Bible where God clearly commands meditation is in Joshua 1:8. What do you think Jesus did, "In the early morning, while it was still dark . . . " (Mark 1:35)? In 1 Timothy 4:15, Paul instructs, "Meditate upon these things"(KJV). But what is meditation? Meditation is simply thought which is prolonged and focused on a single object. It is:

- **Chewing,** like a cow chews—in and out for more grinding.
- **Analyzing**—taking the good, long look; also polishing, like polishing glasses to see more clearly.
- . **Acting**—turning words to thoughts and thoughts to action, thus involving life. According to Richard Foster meditation is "the ability to hear God's voice and obey his word."[1]

While Eastern religions primarily meditate to empty or cleanse the mind, Christians meditate in order to fill the cleansed mind with the things of God. Meditation is not an end in itself. It is a means to an end and must always be linked very closely to prayer. Prayer is like a fountain which rises out of an underground reservoir of meditation—meditation upon God and God's will.

Calvin Miller helps us put Christian meditation in perspective:

> Inner silence is easiest to achieve in a place of outer silence. This is the prayer closet that Jesus spoke of in Matthew 6. Here we shut out as much human intercourse as possible. Yet, we are never to pursue inwardness. We are to pursue Christ. There is no power in meditative systems that clear the heart but cannot refill it with substance. In my years of studying Eastern religion, I discovered that many devotees of yoga cleanse their minds but leave them empty. Soon their minds fill with the same sort of congestion which had just been swept away.[2]

Several warnings are fitting related to meditation. Beware of getting alone with your own thoughts. Get alone with God's thoughts. Don't meditate upon yourself, but dwell on God. There is always a danger in meditating on problems. Reflect on Scripture and seek answers to problems. Remember this is *musement* not *amusement.* Muse was a Greek god who spent time in solitude and thinking. "Amuse" may keep us from concentrating on God.

Meditating in the Psalms:
Psalm 63:6
Psalm 119:15
Psalm 119:78
Psalm 119:98
Psalm 119:148
Psalm 1:2
Psalm 19:14

These suggestions may make meditation more meaningful:

- Emphasize different words within a passage of scripture.
- Ask questions (who, what, where, when, why, how) of the passage.
- Apply the passage to your life by asking such questions as: What truth should I gain from this; should I eliminate anything from my life after reading this passage; should I change anything in my life after reading this passage; should I begin anything new after reading this passage.
- Translate or paraphrase the passage into your own words.

Among the benefits of meditation is the value of memorizing scripture. As you meditate on a passage of scripture over and over, it will find its way into your memory.

Experiencing spiritual unction or anointing is another benefit, as seen in the following statement by E. M. Bounds, the great prayer warrior and author:

> Unction comes . . . not in the study but in the closet. It is heaven's distillation in answer to prayer. It is the sweetest exhalation of the Holy Spirit. It . . . softens . . . cuts and soothes. It carries the Word like dynamite, like salt, like sugar; makes the Word a soother, an arranger, a revealer, a searcher; makes the hearer . . . weep like a child and live like a giant. This unction is not found in the halls of learning. . . . It is the gift of God. It is heaven's knighthood given to the chosen true and brave ones who have sought this anointed honor through many an hour of tearful, wrestling prayer.[3]

Another benefit of meditation comes when we allow it to affect all the senses. What do we see, hear, feel, smell, and taste related to a passage of scripture?

A final benefit of meditation is empowering. If we desire power for any activity to which God calls us—be it vocational ministry, secular work, personal concerns, family concerns, or crisis coping—we can get it through prayer.

The *I* implies Intercession as demonstrated in 1 Samuel 12:23, Genesis 18:23-33, Numbers 14:13-19, John 17, Ephesians 3:14-21, and Hebrews 7:23-25. Intercession is always for other people. We supplicate and petition for self; we intercede for others. Indeed the scripture says, "Far be it from me that I should sin against the Lord by ceasing to pray for you" (1 Sam. 12:23). One authority says intercession "means that according to God's will man in and through prayer may be privileged to share in the unfolding of God's purpose."[4] Intercession, then, is a conference with God to communicate about someone else.

Showing the importance of intercession to God, two-ninths of the prayer in the Bible, where we know the answer, is petition prayer (for the person praying) while seven-ninths is intercession (for others). In the Old Testament, the prophets and kings of Israel often pleaded for their people before God (see sidebar). In the New - Testament the intercessory prayer ministry of Jesus is highlighted, as is Paul's. Paul also encouraged Christians to intercede for all people (1 Tim. 2:1-2).

Is it ever out of place to offer intercessory prayer to God? Only when God tells us not to intercede. This happened in Jeremiah's time. So pagan were the worship practices of Israel and so unacceptable were the actions of the people, that God instructed Jeremiah, "Do not pray for this people, and do not lift up cry or prayer for them, and do not intercede with Me; for I do not hear you" (Jer. 7:16). However, unless God instructs you otherwise, as was the case with Jeremiah, intercession is always appropriate.

Old Testament examples of intercession:

Exodus 32:11–14
1 Samuel 12:7ff.
2 Kings 19:14–19
1 Chronicles 21:16–17
Lamentations 5
Daniel 9:16

Today the real intercessors are the men and women of secret influence in all communities. To be mentioned in their prayers is profoundly more beneficial than to be mentioned in their wills. The power of intercessory prayer was shown in a recent study published in the *Southern Medical Journal* and the *Journal of the American Medical Association*. Half of 393 heart patients were randomly assigned to an experimental group. Their health was prayed for by three-to-seven born-again Christians. The other half, the control group, did not receive such prayers. Patients were not told which group they were in. Those praying were given only first names and diagnoses of the patients along with pertinent updates of their condition. Both groups were equally sick when they entered the hospital. The results were patients who were prayed for had fewer complications during their stay in the hospital.[5]

In a similar study, psychologists at the St. Louis University School of Medicine analyzed studies conducted over the past thirty years on the direct effects of intercessory prayer on physical health. In one study, eighteen children with leukemia were divided into two groups. Families from a Protestant church in another city were asked to pray daily for ten of the eighteen children. Fifteen months later, seven of the ten children for whom the church members prayed were still alive, and only two of the eight children in the control group were alive.[6]

So often does intercessory prayer encounter health-related requests, some guidelines are in order. In praying for the health of another, remember that God is a healing God. If we pray, seek God's face, and turn from our wicked ways, God promises to hear from heaven, forgive our sin, and "heal" our land (2 Chron. 7:14). Earlier God had offered this self description:"I, the Lord, am your healer" (Exod. 15:26). Jesus came to earth with a healing ministry as seen in Matthew 4:24, and other places.

Remember that God used specific believers as instruments for divine healing. The emphasis is on *divine healing*, not on *divine healers*. Both

New Testament examples of intercession:

Romans 8:34
Hebrews 7:25
Hebrews 9:24
1 John 2:1–2
Ephesians 6:18
Romans 1:9
Philippians 1:3–4

Elijah and Elisha were used by God as mediums of healing. Jesus instructed his disciples to "Heal the sick" (Matt. 10:8); he shared the same encouragement to a larger group of followers in Luke 10:9.

You can be assured that throughout church history, God's people have prayed for the healing of others and God has responded. Paul describes healing as one of the ministries of the church (1 Cor. 12) and James gives clear instructions to the church to pray for healing (James 5:13-16). I, myself, am living proof of the healing ministry of intercessory prayer, but I must remember and caution, ours is the ministry of intercession for healing; God's is the ministry of healing in response to intercession.

The key to intercessory prayer, then, is to feel the freedom to ask the loving Father for the desires of our heart all the while agreeing that our desires must be set aside to meet the specifications of a higher will should God so decide.

The *G* in MIGHTY implies Giving up. Giving up includes, among other things, the discipline of fasting. This is God's chosen way to deepen and strengthen our prayer life.[7]

The biblical basis for fasting is seen in forty-four references to fasting in the Old Testament and thirty-one in the New Testament (see sidebar).

Among the historical evidences of fasting are references to fasting in the lives of Francis of Assisi, Martin Luther, John Calvin, John Knox, John Wesley, R. A. Torrey, David Brainerd, Jonathan Edwards, Charles G. Finney, Dwight L. Moody, and Billy Graham.

Modern fasting has been described as not looking upon the material necessities of life as unclean, but rather concentrating more on worshiping God in prayer. Thus, for a time, we set aside those things which are both allowable and needed. Perhaps Andrew Murray said it best in his book *The Believer's School of Prayer*: "Prayer needs fasting for its full growth....Prayer is the one hand with which we grasp the invisible; fasting, the other, with which we let loose and cast away the visible."[8]

Fasting is unpopular. We prefer feasting. Fasting is any deliberate self-denial or abstinence for the sole purpose of growing spiritually stronger and enhancing the work of the kingdom of God. Specifically, in the Bible fasting refers to abstaining from food for spiritual purposes. Indeed, "In fasting, a believing people acknowledge to God that the urgent concerns of the spiritual take precedence over the normal concerns of the physical."[9] It can be abused; however, this is not the real danger. The real danger is in missing the blessing.

Fasting is not a means by which you earn God's blessing and God's answer to prayer. Further, it is not a way to bypass obedience, nor is it an automatic way to secure a miracle. Fasting does not accumulate power to your heavenly account, so that you can display it at your pleasure.

How, then, should you fast properly? Here are some suggestions. Keep in mind the purpose of fasting—to please God (Zech. 7:5). Understand that the call to fast is from God (Joel 1:14; 2:15; Luke 5:33-35). Realize that fasting is a humbling experience before God because it includes repentance (1 Kings 21:27; Ps. 35:13; 1 Pet. 5:6). Fasting is not a substitute for obedience (Isa. 58:3-5). Avoid fasting legalistically, for when it becomes mostly form and ritual, it becomes devoid of meaning. Vary the times of fasting (one-half day, one day, several days). Employ good medical advice before serious fasting. Fast for one meal as a beginning and spend that time and additional time if possible in prayer. Avoid strenuous exercise while fasting. Keep fasting as a matter between you and God. If you must tell, give God the glory.

Arthur Wallis helps us understand various forms of fasting:

Among those who fasted are:

Moses (Deut. 9:9, 18; Exod. 34:28)
Joshua (Josh. 7:6)
David (Ps. 35:13)
Jehoshaphat (2 Chron. 20:3)
Daniel (Dan. 10:3)
Elijah (1 Kings 19:8)
Anna (Luke 2:36-38)
Jesus (Matt. 4:2)
Paul (Acts 14:23, 9:9)
Church leaders in Antioch (Acts 13:2-3).

1. normal fast (Matt. 4:2, no solid or liquid other than water)
2. absolute fast (Acts 9:9, same as normal fast but no water; normally this lasted for three days at most)
3. partial fast (Dan. 10:3, diet restriction)
4. regular fast (Jer. 36:6, also Day of Atonement and Luke 18:11-12, twice per week at a set time)
5. public fast (Joel 2:15, could be "regular" or called)[10]

In *Celebration of Discipline*, Richard Foster adds a sixth form of fasting:

6. supernatural fasting (Deut. 9:9; 1 Kings 19:8)

Rather than see fasting as simply related to food and drink, we need to broaden the definition. O. Hallesby helps us:

> Fasting is not confined to abstinence from eating and drinking. Fasting really means voluntary abstinence for a time from various necessities of life, such as food, drink, sleep, rest, association with people and so forth. . . . Fasting in the Christian sense does not involve looking upon the necessities of life, which we have mentioned, as unclean or unholy. . . . Fasting implies merely that our souls at certain times need to concentrate more strongly on the one thing needful than at other times, and for that reason we renounce for the time being those things which in themselves, may be both permissible and profitable.[11]

Andy Anderson, after a five-year search, listed several spiritual benefits in his own life from fasting.

1. I am spiritually cleaned.
2. I have learned a new discipline.
3. I have discovered a more effective prayer life.
4. I have found a previously unknown peace and confidence.
5. I have found an almost unbelievable strength to overcome temptations.[12]

The spiritual benefits far outweigh the physical benefits of fasting, but we must not neglect them. Stormie Omartian lists for us fourteen physical benefits that are part of the extra blessing God gives when we submit to God through fasting (see sidebar).

Following his forty-day fast, Bill Bright, founder of Campus Crusade for Christ International, wrote, "Nothing can compare with fasting and prayer to bring personal revival and renewal to the church. I believe the next move of God, which is now under way, will restore biblical fasting to the body of Christ."[14]

The *H* in MIGHTY implies Humbling ourselves, as demonstrated in 2 Chronicles 7:14. In this verse the proper order is seen ("My people who are called by My name humble themselves and pray . . .") as humbling properly precedes prayer. When we put prayer ingredients in priority then the word of the psalmist is activated: "He does not forget the cry of the humble" (Ps. 9:12 NKJV).

The joy of praying with a humble spirit is often poisoned by pride. Pride and humility do not mix. Pride drives us from God but humility draws us to God. Pride puffs us up while humility brings us down. Pride makes us high minded while humility makes us people of low degree. Pride keeps us from prayer while humility drives us to prayer.

Thus a humble spirit and an effective prayer life go together. Again the psalmist exclaims, "O Lord, You have heard the desire of the humble; You will strengthen their heart, You will incline Your ear" (Ps. 10:17). God loves to hear and respond

Fourteen physical benefits of fasting:

1. Establishing self-control
2. Curbing and eventually eliminating cravings and bad habits
3. Slowing the aging process
4. Adding strength
5. Causing the body to consume excess fat
6. Eliminating body odor and bad breath
7. Giving clear skin and bright eyes
8. Eliminating chronic fatigue
9. Clearing up foggy or fuzzy thinking
10. Elevating self-esteem and promoting a sense of well-being
11. Relieving stress, tension, and anxiety
12. Saving on food bills
13. Causing better sleep patterns
14. Ensuring that you'll feel and look better.[13]

to the prayer of one whose heart is not filled with pride but whose life is directed by humility. These are the people who remind the Father of the Son who "humbled Himself by becoming obedient . . . " (Phil. 2:8).

How would you like for your name to appear on the following list of people who were humble in their communication with God:

- Abraham (Gen. 18:27)
- Moses (Exod. 3:11)
- David (2 Sam. 7:18)
- Solomon (1 Kings 3:7)
- Isaiah (Isa. 6:5)
- Jeremiah (Jer. 1:6)
- Daniel (Dan. 2:30)
- Mary (Luke 1:38)
- John the Baptist (John 1:27)
- Paul (Eph. 3:8)

To even be considered in the same breath with these greats is humbling, yet you can be added to this list if you humble yourself before God.

It was about this spirit of humbling ourselves that Lenny LeBlanc and Greg Gulley wrote in *No Higher Calling*:

> Down at Your feet, Oh Lord
> Is the most high place
> In Your presence, Lord
> I seek Your face
> I seek Your face
> There is no higher calling
> No greater honor
> Than to bow and kneel
> Before Your throne
> I'm amazed at Your glory
> Embraced by Your mercy
> Oh Lord, I live to worship You

The *T* in MIGHTY implies Travail. While all prayer is fulfilling and most prayer is joyful, some prayer includes exhausting travail. Travail in general means physical hard work, toil, labor, and even agony. Similarly, prayer travail is physically, emotionally, and spiritually draining. It is spiritual wrestling, sometimes called importunity, that affects our whole being.

Hezekiah and Isaiah travailed in prayer as they "cried out to heaven" (2 Chron. 32:20). The Sons of Israel "cried again" to God in confession of sin (Neh. 9:28). When Hannah prayed, she was "greatly distressed" and "wept bitterly" (1 Sam. 1:10). Even our Lord "offered up both prayers and supplications with loud crying and tears" (Heb. 5:7). Many others travailed in prayer as well (see sidebar).

Travail is the third level of praying that Jesus described in Matthew 7:7 when he instructed his disciples to "ask," "seek," and "knock." Asking is a simple, basic form of prayer. Seeking is a bit more intense involving more earnestness and perseverance. Knocking is urgent, often desperate work. It is prayer travail.

So intensely did Jesus travail in prayer in Gethsemane that "His sweat became like drops of blood" (Luke 22:44). While our prayer agony will never reach the level of our Lord's Garden travail, he must forever be our model in prayer. How long has it been since you have travailed in Christlike prayer?

Phrases like "wrestling in prayer," "agonizing in prayer," and "striving in prayer" were common in the early church and in the lives of great prayer warriors

Scriptures showing "travailing" prayers:

Exodus 2:23–24
Nehemiah 1:4
Job 23:1–4
Psalm 6:4–6
Psalm 35:13–14
Psalm 38:9–10
Psalm 39:12
Psalm 55:1–2
Psalm 88:9
Psalm 102:5
Lamentations 2:18–19
Daniel 10:12
Joel 2:12
Zechariah 12:10
John 11:38–42
Romans 8:26

throughout history. In referring to prayer for the believers in Colosse, Paul writes, "I want you to know how great a struggle I have on your behalf" (Col. 2:1) and writing about one of their own, Paul describes Epaphras as "always laboring earnestly for you in his prayers" (Col. 4:12). Additionally Paul urged the believers in Rome, "Strive together with me in your prayers to God for me ... " (Rom. 15:30).

Just as Monica travailed in tears before God for the salvation of her son Augustine, and Martin Luther travailed before God for the healing of his friend Melanchthon, and Ann Judson travailed with God when her husband, Adoniram Judson, was imprisoned in Burma, so we must learn to travail in prayer. P. T. Forsyth wrote:

> Lose the importunity of prayer, reduce it to soliloquy, or even colloquy, with God, lose the real conflict of will, lose the habit of wrestling and the hope of prevailing with God, make it mere walking with God in friendly talk; and, precious as that is, yet you tend to lose the reality of prayer at last.[15]

While prayer must include both submission and travail, I remind you that it was only after much agonizing, striving, and pleading in the Garden that Jesus prayed "Your will be done" (Matt. 26: 42). So let us persist in prayer, travailing before God.

The *Y* implies Yielding as demonstrated in Gethsemane when Jesus yielded to the decision of the Father. After supplication and even travail, our Lord yielded with the words, "Nevertheless, not as I will, but as You will" (Matt. 26:39 NKJV).

Obviously, yielding in prayer comes as a result of the greater yielding of life. If we surrender all, yield all, and give God all, then yielding in prayer becomes a part of the overall pattern of life. Only after you have yielded to the "Father who is in heaven," can you adequately pray, "Your will be done" (Matt. 6:9–10).

While in London, J. Wilbur Chapman had the opportunity to meet General William Booth, founder of The Salvation Army. After listening reverently to the General's stories, the American evangelist asked Booth for the secret of his success. Booth spoke briefly of how, as a boy, he had knelt at a bare table in the schoolroom of

Nottingham's Broad Street Chapel and made a vow with God. Booth concluded, "I will tell you the secret. God has had all there was of me." Years later his daughter added to her father's answer, "That wasn't really his secret—his secret was that he never took it back." Yielding to God is giving all and not taking it back.

On one occasion, D. L. Moody had a conversation with another well-known evangelist of their day, Henry Varley. Seated in a public park in Dublin, Varley said to Moody, "The world has yet to see what God will do with and for and through and in and by the man who is fully consecrated to Him." After reflecting on these words, Moody determined to be that man.

The world would say if you yield to God like that, you will surely suffer. However, yielding does not always mean that we will receive less from God than we have petitioned. We may get exactly what we ask and no more. I recall a seminary student boldly asking God to give him a certain number of public decisions in an upcoming revival meeting. He obviously did not complement his request with a "nevertheless." At the conclusion of the third revival service, the requested number of decisions had been recorded. Then for the remainder of the week-long meeting, no further decisions were made. Failure to yield to God's will meant, in this case, limiting God. Complete yielding might have been the occasion for God to pour out blessings on the student preacher and the church.

Request of God the "desires of your heart" (Ps. 37:4), then, like Jesus, yield by praying, "Nevertheless, Thy will be done." Even delayed yielding is better than no yielding even though the cost of the delay is often overwhelming.

Baptist hymn writer B. B. McKinney wrote of the yielding ingredient of prayer as follows:

> Speak to my heart, Lord Jesus,
> Speak that my soul may hear;
> Speak to my heart, Lord Jesus,
> Calm every doubt and fear.
> Speak to my heart, oh speak to my heart,
> Speak to my heart, I pray;

Yielded and still, seeking Thy will,
Speak to my heart today.
Speak to my heart, Lord Jesus,
It is no longer mine;
Speak to my heart, Lord Jesus,
I would be wholly Thine.
Speak to my heart, oh, speak to my heart,
Speak to my heart, I pray;
Yielded and still, seeking Thy will,
Oh, speak to my heart today.

When you pray beyond the basic ingredients, it's time to take on additional responsibility and be a praying-in-public prayer-shaped disciple.

14. Private to Public Prayer:
Will You Lead Us?

Many who faithfully pray in private have problems when called on to pray in public. We must move beyond this to a balance of private and public praying. This need to balance private prayer with public prayer is addressed by Korean pastor Paul Y. Cho:

> As a tree has its root hidden in the ground and its stem growing up into the sunlight, so prayer needs secrecy in which the soul meets God alone and public fellowship with those who find their common meeting place in the Name of Jesus.[1]

Groups in New Testament days were not large according to our standards today. However, there is an example of public prayer within a large group in Acts. After Peter and John had been released from prison, they told their story to the believers gathered together. In response, "They lifted their voices to God with one accord" (Acts 4:24). The fact is God does much work in response to public prayer.

However, there is an added responsibility in public prayer which does not exist in private prayer. In public prayer the one praying has the responsibility of leading the entire group before God. For this reason the one presiding should give careful attention to the person on whom he or she calls to lead. As a young pastor, I called on a particular man to lead our service in a closing prayer. As we all bowed our heads, he said, "No!" Embarrassed, I led the prayer. Later, I discovered that this particular man never led in public prayer. It awakened me early in my ministry to some of the challenges of helping people learn their responsibilities related to public prayer.

To increase the effectiveness of public praying, one must sometimes be critical. But criticizing public prayer is a dangerous thing to do. More often than not, the critic seems to offend the one who needs the constructive criticism. Lehman Strauss commented:

> Oh, those public prayers! Some of them are said in dead language fit for no environment except a cemetery. But because they are prayers, the man is wrong who criticizes them.[2]

Please understand that when you lead in prayer during a worship service, you are doing more than just communicating with God for yourself. You are leading a group of people in communication with God, voicing the prayer on their behalf. Public prayers all too often are little more than a series of religious phraseology and when this happens the serious accusation made by Theodore Jennings may be true:

> People learn to be atheists not from too much contact with the world, but from too much contact with the church. No number of closely reasoned proofs for the existence of God will ever overcome the impression gained Sunday after Sunday that our prayers are addressed to ourselves.[3]

So don't talk to the people before God nor talk to God while ignoring the people. Rather, lead the people as you and they talk with God.

Generally there are three kinds of public prayer. The first of these is liturgical prayer. These are always read and most often from previously written prayers. They are formal and specific to the point.

To the other extreme in public worship are spontaneous prayers—that is, no prior announcement is given. The person who is to lead is simply called on by surprise and is expected to lead pray for the needs of the group.

Both of these extremes leave something to be desired. While neither should be avoided, perhaps the balance between the two comes through extemporaneous prayers.

In extemporaneous praying, a forewarning is given to the person who will do the praying. This gives opportunity for some thoughtful preparation and at the same time, allows for some spontaneity. One danger is praying without a moment's pause to think about what we're going to say. Wait awhile until you have focused your own mind, and then when you clearly know yourself what you want to do, you will be able to lead the group.

I shall always appreciate a former minister who came to me during the meal time, before a Wednesday evening prayer service, and asked permission to call upon me to pray for those on the hospital list. During the meal, I was able to review this hospital list. As the prayer meeting started I listened attentively to the mention of many new names that were not on my list. When the minister finally called upon me to pray, I'm sure I did a better job than if my prayers had been spontaneous. My prayers were thought out and focused.

To make public prayer more effective, you should be aware of these principles:

1. Be brief and to the point. If it is an offertory prayer, you should pray primarily for the offering. This is not time to catch up on your prayer life or to repeat clichés. As one preacher said, "Sentence prayers are not meant to be life sentences."

2. Avoid "stained-glass vocabulary." Lead the people to God in language that the people understand. In leading public prayer, you should not try to impress the group with a spiritual vocabulary different from normal speech. In other words, "thee" and "thou" should be discarded in favor of more current language. As a teenager on a prayer retreat, I made a commitment to talk to God in normal language. Because I started early, I was able to work the "stained-glass vocabulary" out of my prayers.

3. Avoid repetition. We do not use repetition in normal conversation, yet we often use it in prayer, sometimes using God's name at both the beginning and the end of each sentence. We also have used catchy phrases which are simply repetitious, such as "each and every one," "lead, guide and direct," and "bless this food to the nourishment of our bodies." Jesus instructed his disciples to avoid display and repetition in prayer (Matt. 6:5–8).

4. Be specific. There was a man in a former church where I served who ended every prayer with the words "bless all those for whom it's our duty to pray." The thought often came to my mind that he was "scatter shooting." Leading public prayer should be specific. Every time I hear "bless all the missionaries," I wonder if God would not like to respond, "Name three . . . who are living." The very word "bless" is not even specific enough. God blessed the Israelites by allowing them to wander in the wilderness for forty years, although they did not see it as "blessing."

5. Pray in a normal tone of voice and at a normal speed. I'll never forget the first meeting of the ministerial alliance which I attended as a freshman in a Baptist college. A student who lived down the hall from me in the dorm led in the opening prayer. I could hardly believe my ears when he spoke at a very fast speed and in a very loud volume. I knew he didn't talk that way in the dorm, and I wondered why he chose to communicate with God that way.

Let's examine the kind of prayers we might offer in a public service of worship. A look at nearly any printed agenda from any church on any given Sunday indicates there are at least six possible kinds of prayers offered in the service: the invocation, the pastoral prayer, the prayer of praise, the offertory prayer, the sermon-related prayer, and the benediction. While these may take on different titles than the ones I list here and while some are merged with other types of prayers, the following list will be helpful in identifying the various kinds.

The *invocation* is usually offered toward the beginning of a worship service and has one basic purpose: to invite and acknowledge the presence of God among those gathered together. In other words, the purpose is to "invoke" because a special and sacred activity is about to begin. It leads the people to look toward God with thanksgiving for the divine presence in their midst and for what is about to happen as they worship. The invocation ought to make mention of one or more names or titles of God as well as make a declaration of our desire to communicate and to be accepted as worthy worshipers.

The *pastoral prayer* is, as its title indicates, a prayer offered by the pastor or senior minister of the congregation. While other prayers in the worship service may be offered by other ministers or laypersons, this particular prayer ought to be offered by the pastor, and it ought to be on an appropriate level with the pastor's sermon. The sermon is the pastor's opportunity to present the Word of God to the people. The pastoral prayer is an opportunity to present the needs of the people to God. Each congregation ought to have the privilege of hearing their pastor talk to God on their behalf. Just as the pastor will spend time studying the Word of God before it is brought to the people, surely comparable time ought to be spent studying the needs of the people before bringing them before God. This pastoral prayer should include an acknowledgment of God's involvement with the congregation. It may also include a corporate confession on behalf of the people (see Isa. 6). The pastoral prayer may focus outward to the circumstances, both local and worldwide, that affect the congregation. Because the pastor knows the people, the pastoral prayer might also focus inward on the needs of the people themselves. The pastor might well pray for activities that are on the calendar in the upcoming days or for particular needs that express themselves in the lives of individuals within the congregation.

A third type of prayer offered in public worship is a *prayer of praise*. For many years this prayer has been absent in public worship but is seemingly making a return. Many congregations delegated this prayer to the choir as they gave a choral response of praise to a worded prayer offered by the pastor or some other person. Indeed, this prayer might well be sung or spoken in unison by the congregation as well as voiced by one person (see Ps. 22:3; 35:18; Heb. 13:15).

The *offertory prayer* is an integral part of the worship experience. It may come before or after the receiving of the offering, depending on the wishes of the congregation and its leaders. This prayer should be taken seriously and should be specifically spoken in relationship to the offering. In other words, this is a time to pray specifically in the area of stewardship, church budget, financial planning, and ministry opportunities beyond the local church level that require church financial investment. The person praying this prayer, often a layperson, such as one of the offering-takers, should be instructed that this is a prayer related to the giving of money to the work of God through the church. This is not an appropriate time to pray the same type prayer that one would pray in an invocation or in a benediction or in a pastoral prayer of intercession. In a church where I served as interim pastor, the following letter was sent each week to the person who would lead the offertory prayer:

> Thank you for agreeing to lead the Offertory Prayer this coming Sunday morning. The following tips should assist you as you prepare and as you pray.
>
> 1. Come to the pulpit during the last line of the song preceding the Offertory Prayer and stand to the side so you can begin praying as soon as we stop singing.
>
> 2. Pray specifically for the offering. This is not an Invocation, nor a Pastoral Prayer. You may want to include thanks for the offerings already given during the Bible Study time. Prayers for the overall stewardship of the church and the use of the offering (missions, evangelistic outreach, benevolence, etc.) are very much in order

3. Speak directly into the microphone. Your prayer is to God but you are also leading the congregation in prayer.

4. It is all right to use a small card with prayer notes, outlines, thoughts, etc. Since you are leading the congregation in prayer, some preparation is needed and notes are in order if you need them.

5. Please take seriously this specific assignment in the worship service. The various parts of the service should flow together to glorify God and edify the people.

A fifth form of worship service prayer is the *sermon-related prayer*. Some ministers prefer to pray this at the beginning of the sermon, perhaps following the reading of the scripture. Here, the minister asks God's blessing on the Word and the sharing of it. Other ministers may prefer to conclude their sermon with a prayer, again asking God to bless the proclaimed Word to the hearing and application of the people. A prayer at the end of the sermon also allows a time of transition to the invitation and response time, and thus might well be a time of personal reflection led by the minister.

A final form of prayer in public worship is the *benediction*. This is the concluding prayer in most worship services. Too often it is merely a signal that the service is over. When this is true, people use this time for the gathering of personal possessions such as coats, umbrellas, Bibles, and printed materials. Some even leave to get an early start from the parking lot or to some other engagement. The benediction is more than simply a closing prayer. It is an acknowledgment of God's blessing on the congregation as they go from the place of worship. Biblical patterns for this benediction can be found in Numbers 6:24-26, 2 Corinthians 13:14, Ephesians 3:20-21, and Jude 24-25.

The centrality and importance of prayer in worship was expressed pointedly by George Buttrick:

Corporate prayer is the heart of corporate worship. Ritual is not central; for, however necessary and vital, it is still ritual. Scripture is not central; for, however indispensable and radiant, it is still scripture—that which is written, the record not the experience, the very word but not the Presence. Preaching is not central; for preaching, however inevitable and kindling, is still preaching—the heralding, not the very Lord. . . . When the rite is made central, prayer may become an incantation. When the Book is made central, prayer may become an appendage of scribal interpretations. When preaching is made central, prayer . . . may become only an introduction and conclusion to the sermon. The heart of religion is in prayer—the uplifting of human hands, the speaking of human lips, the expectant waiting of human silence—in direct communion with the Eternal. Prayer must go through the rite, scripture, symbolism, and sermon, as light through a window.[4]

Several years ago an article appeared in *Eternity* magazine entitled, "The Ten Most Unwanted Public Prayer Habits." This was a humorous look at how we have fallen into bad habits. The ten are listed below with brief comment from the article:

1. The solemn assembly prayer—this prayer begins when the person praying drops his voice an entire octave in order to sound more sacred.
2. The cliché camouflage—this occurs when the person praying fills the prayer with as many religious clichés as possible.
3. The prayer of the just—this prayer is prayed when the person praying uses the word "just" throughout the prayer.
4. The holy promotion—the prayer is offered to raise support for a particular activity or project.
5. The lecture prayer—in this prayer the minister lectures the congregation on subjects too explosive to cover in the sermon.
6. The Father Father prayer—in this prayer the person praying uses the word Father or some other word for God over and over as at the beginning and ending of each phrase.
7. The you know syndrome, you know—in this prayer the person praying feels compelled to remind God of all the things

God knows and repeats the phrase "you know" over and over in the prayer.

8. The round-the-world prayer—during this prayer the person praying feels compelled to mention every opportunity of which he is aware and perhaps even every missionary that he knows by name.

9. The payment-on-demand prayer—in this prayer the person praying attempts to hold God accountable for every single promise in the scripture. The phrase often occurs in this prayer, "Lord you have promised . . . "

10. In conclusion, the summary prayer—during this prayer the minister summarizes the entire worship service, particularly the sermon just preached and may even include a summary of the points to the sermon.[5]

While the one who prays in public bears a heavy responsibility, so does each member of the group or congregation. Stanley J. Grenz gives the following suggestions for the congregation:

- assume a reverent attitude when another begins to pray
- be conscious of the nearness of God during the prayer time
- listen to the prayer sympathetically, as one who is also standing before God in prayer
- during the time of public prayer take ownership over the prayer being voiced
- listen to the voice of God during the prayer
- use this occasion as a basis for celebration.[6]

In the public praise offered because of the release of Peter and John, the scripture says, "And when they heard this, they lifted their voices to God in one accord" (Acts 4:24). The idea "of one accord" means to pray in a concert of desire and will. It does not necessarily mean to all pray at the same time, for that could easily be discord. The idea of "voices" means many praying in agreement and in affirmation with one voice praying aloud. In this particular passage the voices may refer to the repeating or singing of the prayer in Psalm 2 which follows

Acts 4:24. This psalm was so well known that the listeners would have easily joined in the quoting when the one praying began to use these words. Jesus prayed that his disciples would be "one" (John 17:21). One place where current disciples of Jesus can demonstrate unity is in praying in one accord for common needs and purposes.

In regard to public prayer, the words of James Montgomery seem especially appropriate:

> They walked with God in Peace and Love,
> But failed with one another
> While sternly for the Faith they strove,
> Brother fell out with brother;
> But He in whom they put their trust,
> Who knew their frames that they were dust,
> Pitied and healed their weakness.
>
> He found them in His House of Prayer,
> With one accord assembled;
> And so revealed His presence there,
> They wept with joy and trembled:
> One cup they drank, one bread they brake,
> One baptism shared, one language spake,
> Forgiving and forgiven.
>
> Then forth they went with tongues of flame,
> In one blest theme delighting;
> The Love of Jesus and His name,
> God's children all uniting;
> That Love our theme and watchword still,
> The law of love may we fulfill,
> And love as we are loved.

Much of public praying is done in the context of the local church. So, it naturally follows that one who practices public prayer, should pray not only while at church functions, but for the church—local and universal.

15. For the Church:
Body Language

However simple it may sound, the church of Jesus Christ becomes a praying church through praying. There are many descriptions and analogies of the church given throughout the Bible. However, on one occasion, speaking to his disciples gathered in a place of worship, Jesus said, "My house will be called a house of prayer" (Isa. 56:7; Matt. 21:13; Mark 11:17; Luke 19:46).

Prior to the New Testament organization of the church, the people of Israel often prayed in "Solemn Assembly." The term "solemn assembly" (translated "sacred assembly" in the NIV) is defined as follows: *solemn*—"performed with religious sanction or tradition"[1]; *assembly*—"a group of persons gathered together, as for worship, instruction, entertainment, etc."[2]; *solemn assembly*—"a term used mainly of the community of Israel gathered and separated for a solemn occasion, whether on a stated day of resting or fasting, or for an extraordinary reason."[3]

The biblical basis for solemn assembly is seen in the Old Testament. Both Leviticus 23:36 ff. and Numbers 28-29 offer lists of prescribed days each year that were to be set aside as holy convocations or solemn assemblies. These included:

1. First day of the Feast of the Passover
2. Seventh day of the Feast of the Passover
3. Feast of Firstfruits
4. Feast of Trumpets
5. Day of Atonement
6. First day of the Feast of Tabernacles
7. Eighth day of the Feast of Tabernacles

Numbers 10:1-10 declared the priests were to blow trumpets and call the people together at the Tent of Meeting. Deuteronomy 16:8 tells us a solemn assembly was the conclusion of Passover. For six days the people were to eat unleavened bread, and on the seventh day, they were to "hold an assembly to the Lord." In 2 Kings 10:20, Jehu called for a solemn assembly for Baal. In 2 Chronicles 7:9, the eighth day of the Feast of Tabernacles was observed by Nehemiah and Ezra. In Joel 1:13-15 and 2:1-17 a solemn assembly was called by Joel for spiritual renewal and consecration. In Zephaniah 3:18, Zephaniah envisioned the Lord calling a solemn assembly after a sorrowful judgment. Other "assemblies" considered to have been "solemn" are:

- Asa's (2 Chronicles 15:9)
- Jehoshaphat's (2 Chronicles 20:1-4)
- Hezekiah's (2 Chronicles 29)
- Josiah's (2 Chronicles 34)
- Ezra's (Ezra 9-10)
- Jeremiah's, announcing judgment (Jeremiah 4:5-21)
- Jeremiah's, warning of judgment (Jeremiah 6:1-17)
- Ezekiel's, warning of judgment (Ezekiel 33:3)
- Hosea's, announcing judgment (Hosea 5:8-15)
- Hosea's, announcing judgment again (Hosea 8:1)

The biblical basis for solemn assemblies is also seen in the New Testament. According to Richard Owen Roberts, "Most professing Christians have never heard of a solemn assembly. Of the relatively small number who have, a substantial portion consider it as merely an Old Testament practice of no particular relevance today."[4]

While the term "solemn assembly" does not appear in the New Testament, the Jewish Christians continued to observe their Old Testament customs. In all probability they were observing some customs during the feasts of Pentecost and Passover in Acts 2 and 12. Preceded by ten days of prayer, the Day of Pentecost brought the coming of the Holy Spirit in Acts 2. In Acts 12, on the seventh day of Passover Week (an Old Testament solemn assembly time), Christians were praying for Peter who had been imprisoned by Herod as a part of the persecution of the church. That night, in the midst of imprisonment, Peter was dramatically released by an act of God in response to the prayers of Christians.

What does this say to us for now? There are several applications of solemn assemblies for our day. One is the application to Sunday worship. While we may not need the legalistic keeping of the Sabbath known to the Pharisees, we do need a new dedication to the sacredness of the Lord's day. We are told early in God's word that God "blessed" this day and "sanctified it" (Gen. 2:3). Then God commanded us to "remember the sabbath day, to keep it holy" (Exod. 20:8). This should be a day of sacred assembly of God's people for worship and spiritual celebration. The events of the week will be better managed if the worship of the Lord's day is better maintained.

A second application relates to renewal and revival. The harvest revivals of our forefathers were set times of renewal. We need times set aside on our church calendar for sacred renewal of our assembly and for asking God to send genuine revival.

A third application for our day comes in the sacrifices and offerings. In a time of relative affluence, we run the same risk as the Hebrews when God warned them in their prosperity, "watch yourself, that you do not forget the Lord" (Deut. 6:12). As we gather in sacred assembly, we need to remember that "all the tithe . . . is the Lord's" (Lev. 27:30). Financial hardship often follows faulty stewardship.

A fourth application is to the entire church family. We need to remember that biblical solemn assemblies were not come-as-you-can occasions but were for the entire assembly. Today's sacred assemblies must touch every member of the church family.

A final application to our day relates to the judgment of God. Entering the holy presence of God always allowed the possibility of judgment on sin and unrighteousness. When churches enter sacred assemblies, they must be able to discern and respond to God's judgment.

The process of organizing a solemn assembly must include planning of the time. Clear the calendar of conflicts within and outside the church. Announce far enough in advance to get it on the calendar of all members. Decide on length. Decide on the place. Reserve a place without conflict and free of interruptions, such as a lock-in format or a retreat center. Clear the meeting place of distractions. Carefully plan the content. Possible activities include scripture reading, prayer, confession, offering, praise, renewal, and personal testimony.

There are several common characteristics of historical solemn assemblies that may to some degree resemble modern ones. Assemblies were preceded by periods of spiritual and sometimes moral decline on the part of God's people and by God's burden on the leadership. The normal or routine was set aside for the special agenda. Consistency gave way to a time of intensity. The entire church body attended. They were times of sacrifice leading to further sacrifice— a time to participate and continue to participate. They were extended seasons of prayer. They were times of corporate repentance (weeping, mourning, and humility). They allowed the younger members to see the older members exercise spiritual leadership and gave God an opportunity to respond to the people as they went before God. Finally, they were times for searching the scriptures for God's message in the midst of their difficulties.

Whether with the Biblical people of God meeting in solemn assembly or with the twenty-first century church, prayer must never cease to be a recognizable priority. One of Satan's great strategies is to overcrowd the church's program calendar to the point that prayer loses its priority. This causes a loss of perspective and power. Indeed, "the history of the Christian church is, more than we know, the history of believing prayer."[5] When New Testament leaders were threatened by the powerful Sanhedrin they, "lifted their voices to God . . ." (Acts 4:24), and when Peter was in prison, "prayer for him was being made fervently by the church to God" (Acts 12:5). While prayer must saturate every area of church life, there are some specific areas where it makes a most significant contribution.

Since the beginning of the organized church in the New Testament, church expansion has been linked to prayer, and the historical church must always be what the early church was after the ascension—a group of believers gathered together to pray. In fact, James Campbell reminds us concerning the church:

> As soon as it was born it began to pray; and it grew in strength and efficiency as its prayer-life developed. Through all its subsequent history, down to the present day, it has abounded in service for the Master when it abounded in prayer, and it has declined in the service of the Master when it has declined in prayer.[6]

The growth of the early church in the Acts of the Apostles was saturated by prayer. Every reference to it was accompanied or closely followed by a reference to prayer. Prior to the events on the day of Pentecost, 120 believers had devoted themselves to pray in one accord (Acts 1:14). After the events of Pentecost, three thousand persons were devoted to prayer (Acts 2:42). Later Peter and John were still practicing the habit of going to the temple at the "hour of prayer" (Acts 3:1). After the release of Peter and John, the early church "lifted their voices to God with one accord" in prayer (Acts 4:24). Still later the church prayed for boldness and miracle-working power (Acts 4:31). Following the selection of seven men of good reputation, the church prayed and "laid their hands on them" (Acts 6:6). Early followers of Christ would recognize their first great missionary when they followed God's instructions to "inquire at the

The Apostle Paul prayed for churches in:

Rome (Rom. 1:8–10)
Corinth (1 Cor. 1:4–9)
Galatia (Gal. 1:3–5)
Ephesus (Eph. 1:15–22; 3:14–19)
Philippi (Phil. 1:3–5)
Colosse (Col. 1:3–5a)
Thessalonica (1 Thess. 1:2–3; 2 Thess. 1:3; 2:13)

house of Judas for a man from Tarsus named Saul, for he is praying" (Acts 9:11). Later in the book of Acts, the church prayed for Peter's release (Acts 12:5), and the church in Antioch prayed for Paul and Barnabas as they sent them out on their mission (Acts 13:3). When Paul arrived at Philippi on his second missionary journey, he went to "a riverside, where we were supposing that there would be a place of prayer" (Acts 16:13).

Even after the record of the early church in the book of Acts and the writings of Paul came to an end, the church continued to be saturated in prayer. Historian Kenneth Scott Latourette reminds us:

> The times of prayer were frequent. In the second century it was the custom, presumably held up as the ideal to all the faithful, to pray at daybreak and nightfall when normally Christians came together for prayers and the singing of songs, and at three other hours of the day—at mid-forenoon, at noon, and at mid-afternoon. We also hear of prayers being enjoined at midnight.[7]

We are reminded that in the third century :

> Origin's orthodoxy was questioned but his instruction on prayer had a major influence on Greek life and thought. Tertullian withdrew from the Catholic church and founded his own sect, but his book on the theology and practice of prayer guided Latin theology and practice for a long while.[8]

As prayer and the church continued to be linked together, we discover in the fourth century the prayerful dedication of edifices for Christian worship, and in the fifth Christian century, Augustine (A.D. 354–430), one of the most important figures in the history of the church, had significant words to say related to prayer and the church.

On one occasion Augustine was reported to have said, "How shall I pray to God? . . . I can pray truly that my heart, where you already have a foothold, may receive more and more of you, until one day the whole of me will be filled with the whole of you."[9]

Moving to the thirteenth century, we find Francis of Assisi (A.D. 1182-1226) sending his disciples out by twos, commissioned in prayer to proclaim peace, repentance, and forgiveness to all men everywhere. Certainly the prayer of Francis of Assisi is one of the most beautiful prayers in the history of the church.

When we reach the sixteenth century, we find John Calvin, among others, stressing prayer as conversation with God. We also find in 1549 an act of uniformity passed by Parliament which required the clergy to use a book of common prayer. The great church historian Kenneth Scott Latourette reminds us that "among the common run of Christians there may have been more of private and group prayer than in preceding periods."[10]

In the nineteenth century, a revival in western Norway gave rise to an organization which, without leaving the state church, built its own prayer houses. And among Christians in the United States, there was the development of midweek meetings for church members, usually under the name of prayer meetings.

During the twentieth century, the church in some parts of the world began to experience declining numbers. Even in churches that experienced growth, much of it was through the baptizing of children and teenagers who were raised in the church as a part of families belonging to that church.

The reasons for this decline during the twentieth century are numerous and complex. One reason may be a decline in time spent in prayer. The church has become everything but a house of prayer— a house of worship, of training, of fellowship, and of recreation. While there is much value in each of these endeavors, Jesus seemed to place a priority on prayer when he said, "My house shall be called a house of prayer" (Matt. 21:13). Oh, we believe in prayer. It appears in the worship bulletin several times. We just don't pray very much. I've been in churches where more attention was given to welcoming the guests and making announcements. The problem lies often with the leadership. One study showed pastors averaging one hour per week in prayer, which figures out to be between eight and nine minutes per day.[11] A more recent study among 572 American pastors (crossing regional, age, and denominational lines) showed that 57 percent prayed less than twenty minutes per day; 34 percent prayed between twenty minutes and one hour; only 9 percent prayed more than one hour per day.[12]

While there was general decline and a numerical plateau for others, some churches experienced phenomenal growth. In *The World's Twenty Largest Churches*, John Vaughan helps us to see the reasons behind their growth. Of the First Baptist Church of Dallas, the following is said:

> In addition to the priority of the Sunday School for growth of First Baptist Church, the pastor attributes the increase to four other factors: prayer, visitation and personal soul winning, meeting felt needs, and preaching the Bible as the word of God.[13]

In describing the Young Nak Presbyterian Church in Seoul, Korea, Vaughan said:

> The 3,750 available seats are filled each Sunday for the prayer meeting at dawn (5:00 A.M.) . . . Traditional Wednesday night prayer services are held at 7:00, and this service, too, is broadcast. Members also conduct a Friday noon prayer meeting.[14]

In regard to the largest church in the world, the Central Gospel Church of Seoul, Korea, we learn:

> Church growth does not result from simple application of specific principles. It is born and nurtured through prayer. Calculations based on the time spent in prayer during regular services reveal that members of Central Church spend 260,000 hours in prayer every month.[15]

It is little wonder that many of the largest churches in the world are located in Korea. Reports say that a new Christian congregation is started there every four hours. At 5:00 A.M. church bells ring to call believers to prayer in over thirty-six thousand churches, seven thousand of which are in Seoul alone. In Korea, the Christian population is growing several times faster than the national population, and six new churches are being built each day.

A more recent study done by the Barna Research Group of growing churches in the United States concluded, "Prayer was one of the foundation stones of ministry . . . the battle cry of the congregation" among these churches.[16] This feeling came about as a result of a four-fold emphasis on prayer:

1. the congregation was exposed to biblical teaching concerning the role of prayer in the Christian life
2. the church leadership modeled prayer as normal and significant behavior in the Christian life
3. the people had learned to celebrate the results of prayer
4. church members were held accountable for prayer[17]

In his book *An Inside Look at 10 of Today's Most Innovative Churches*, Elmer Towns describes the prayer ministries of the following:

Skyline Wesleyan Church, San Diego, Ca.—The pastor meets with his 100 Prayer Partners once a month on Saturday morning for prayer and discipleship training. The men are divided into four teams, and each Sunday a different team meets . . . for prayer before the first worship service . . . Then during each morning service the group of men gather in a room above the pulpit to intercede. . . .[18]

The Church on the Way, Van Nuys, Ca.—The morning worship also includes what (Pastor Jack) Hayford calls "ministry time." At this stage, attention is focused on the interaction of the body, with people praying in small groups. Ministry time takes about twelve to fifteen minutes, with some four to five minutes spent in actual prayer.[19]

Second Baptist Church, Houston, Tx.—To demonstrate the extent of their commitment, someone is praying at the church twenty-four hours a day, seven days a week, 365 days a year . . . Twice each month a one-hour prayer orientation is held, teaching new members how to work and pray in the Prayer Room.[20]

In a recent prayer study of Wesleyan church pastors, it was determined that "without exception, growing churches and their pastors show a stronger commitment to prayer ministries. . . . In every category, churches that grew in morning worship attendance for the past two years had a more active prayer ministry."[21]

The effect of prayer in remote churches is likewise impressive. After seventy years of church planting and mission work, the only visible fruit of ministry among the Tarahumara people in the Mexican state of Chihuahua was one struggling congregation of about twenty members. After the *Global Prayer Digest* ran a story on this work, Christians around the world began to pray for church expansion among the Tarahumaras. Twelve years later, there were at least five hundred believers in fifteen congregations and evangelistic work going on in sixteen other villages. The difference? Primarily, prayer![22]

While prayer is closely linked to the world's largest churches, it is by no means de-emphasized in churches that are not considered among the world's largest. In many larger than average churches, we are seeing such things as full-time ministers of prayer on the church staff, prayer towers being built or prayer rooms being designed, full or partial intercessory prayer ministries being coordinated, complete with occasional prayer retreats away from the church location. In medium-sized churches there are prayer rooms and prayer ministries, usually coordinated by a part-time staff member or a volunteer. Even in the smallest of churches, there is a vital link between the health of the church and prayer. In fact, some of the greatest prayer warriors to be found are in the very small churches where no organized prayer ministry exists. Indeed churches of all sizes would be much better off if more time and emphasis was given to prayer. If some church members would spend more time praying and less time criticizing, their churches would be healthier and happier.

More and more churches of all sizes are establishing prayer rooms for the purpose of organized, systematic praying. A church must first decide if it will really support a prayer room. Few things are more revealing on the poor health of a church than a finely adorned, unused prayer room. Don't design one because some other church has one or "everybody's doing it." Prayer rooms result from ongoing prayer ministries; they don't often create them. Once a decision has been made to establish a prayer room, visit other prayer rooms for ideas and suggestions. Many churches have learned both difficult and valuable lessons that could be passed on to you. Either a volunteer or a paid staff member should be assigned the responsibility of coordinating the prayer room ministry. They can then enlist and train intercessors, and it can begin to serve the greater ministry of the healthy church.

Less complicated methods may suffice for your church. Churches of all sizes have had great success with programs such as: prayer chains, prayer telephone lines, computer prayer bulletin boards, prayer links, days of prayer, home or cell prayer meetings, prayer triplets, secret prayer partners, and watchmen-on-the-wall prayer links. The question under consideration is "why?" The answer is that prayer is a divinely ordained, biblically-based, humanly-needed, historically-proven necessity for the growth of a healthy church. Once the "why" question is answered, the "how" question has many answers. Those committed to praying for the church will find ways to do so.

One of the major characteristics of a growing, healthy church is exciting, relevant worship. Believers should be praying regularly for the corporate worship services of churches. Pray that the time spent in worship would glorify God and edify God's people. Pray that Jesus will be lifted up through various means of worship and because of this, the Holy Spirit will draw nonbelievers to God. Pray for guidance for those who plan and direct the worship experience—not just the visible ones but others such as sound technicians and those who care for the children while parents attend the worship service. Pray that worshipers will depart to serve, motivated by their renewed relationship with God. If your church has a printed worship bulletin, spend a few moments before the service begins, praying through this. Ask God to use specific elements of worship to minister to you and others present. Pray that guests, especially those who are spiritually seeking and struggling, will be touched by the worship experience. Understand, there is a marked and measurable difference in worship that is saturated in prayer verses that which is neglected in prayer.

Pray for your pastor, and be certain of at least one thing: your pastor will be appreciative. Remind the pastor of your prayerful support without being overbearing on the pastoral schedule. A brief note or phone message will be an encouragement. Pastors, more than any one else, understand the pressure to lead a healthy and growing church where worship is relevant and fellowship is uplifting. Your prayer support will be an invaluable ingredient to the formula that God blesses for your church.

Perhaps Leonard Ravenhill best describes the difference between healthy churches that are experiencing growth and those that have experienced plateaus or declines:

> The church has many organizers, but few agonizers; many who pay, but few who pray; many resters, but few wrestlers; many who are enterprising, but few who are interceding. People who are not praying are playing.
>
> Two prerequisites of dynamic Christian living are vision and passion. Both of these are generated by prayer. The ministry of preaching is open to a few. The ministry of praying is open to every child of God.
>
> The secret of praying is praying in secret. A worldly Christian will stop praying; a praying Christian will stop worldliness.
>
> Tithes may build the church, but tears will give it life. That is the difference between the modern church and the early church. Our emphasis is on paying; theirs was on praying. When we have paid the place is taken. When they had prayed the place was shaken.
>
> In the matter of effective praying, never have so many left so much to so few. Brethren, let us pray.[23]

But the church will survive and grow and be victorious. It is God's church, the bride Jesus, and when the bridegroom returns in glory, the bride will be waiting. James M. Campbell asks a valid question and shares valuable insight:

> O, where are kings and empires now,
>   Of old that went and came?
>
> But Lord, thy church is praying yet,
>   A thousand years the same.

If the church is fulfilling its normal function, it is growing by reaching out to nonbelievers and assimilating them into its fellowship. Likewise, if a prayer-shaped disciple is praying for the church, the natural continuation of that prayer is for evangelism.

16. For Evangelism:
As You Go ... Pray

Reading of the Acts of the Apostles, you will easily note the evangelistic growth of the early church. The expansion of the church was accompanied by extraordinary praying. This is the type of praying that must be returned to the people of the pews, but we must pray beyond the pews and walls to the multitudes of those who don't know Jesus Christ as Savior and Lord.

Since ultimately all evangelistic activity seeks to "make disciples of all the nations" (Matt. 28:19), it is met with intense resistance by Satan. Effective evangelism is carried out in a climate of warfare, hence the intense need for intercessory prayer.

Prayer and evangelism must be linked together for several reasons. The first is that the Bible speaks concerning this partnership when it says we should "pray the Lord of the harvest to send out laborers into His harvest" (Luke 10:2 NKJV). In setting an example for us, the Apostle Paul asked that his fellow believers "pray for us that the word of the Lord will spread rapidly and be glorified" (2 Thess. 3:1). We ought not only pray for laborers to be sent into the harvest, but we ought to be laborers in the harvest, praying consistently for the unhindered spread of the Gospel.

Second, we ought to link prayer and evangelism because of the current situation. While in 1900, 34.4 percent of the world was Christian, in 1995, 33.7 percent of the world was Christian.[1] We are not winning the world, we are losing it. Also, evangelical Christians have recently lost much of their credibility in the world because of the moral and ethical failures of key Christian leaders. Additionally, the population of the world is growing more rapidly than Christians are able to evangelize and growing in parts of the world where Christian witness is either weak or nonexistent.

There are several times when the need to link prayer and evangelism is more obvious than other times. We should pray for evangelism when:

- Our spiritual depth is shallow—when there is little desire for prayer or Bible study or worship or fellowship with other believers.
- Our church involvement has become apathetic—when our singing is without meaning, when our worship is dull, when there is no praise or celebration in our relationship to God.
- Our compassion is lacking—when there is no genuine desire for renewal in our life, when brokenness is unheard of and when the lostness of individuals is ignored.
- Our witnessing activity diminishes—when there is no emphasis on witnessing, no training in witnessing, no motivation toward witnessing.
- Our priorities get out of order—when the emphasis is on something other than evangelism.
- Our genuine repentance is lacking—genuine repentance and forgiveness precede every significant evangelistic endeavor.

As we look at the connection between prayer and evangelism, it becomes obvious that prayer paves the way for personal evangelism. We should never talk with people about God until we have talked with God about the people. Let no one conclude that prayer is a discipline unrelated to evangelism, for no Christian can move people toward God until they have first been moved by God toward people.

Acts 1:8 implies that we are not to pray to be a witness, because we already are a witness. When the Holy Spirit came to us in conversion, we became a witness. Our proper prayer related to personal evangelism is that we would be sensitive to opportunities to bear witness rather than asking God if we ought to witness.

Further, in Acts 4:29 there is a request for "confidence" or "boldness" in witnessing. This word may also be translated "plainness of speech." Again, we are not to ask God whether or not we should witness, but ask for boldness or plainness of speech in our witness. In these verses and others, we see the truth that prayer paves the way for our involvement in personal evangelism.

Even though the instructions to pray related to being a witness are clear in the scriptures, many believers do not follow them. I often wonder why we spend so much time in our services praying for people who have physical, emotional, and material problems and so little time praying for people with spiritual problems such as lostness. One group of needs is temporal and the other is eternal. Listen to a church pray, and you will know where that church's priorities lie.

Not only does the Bible instruct us to pray related to personal witness, it gives us many specific areas in which to pray:

1. Claim God's desire that none should perish but all should come to repentance (2 Pet. 3:9).
2. Pray that the Holy Spirit would draw the non-Christian to God (John 6:44).
3. Pray that the nonbeliever would seek to know God (Acts 17:27; Deut. 4:29).
4. Pray that the nonbeliever would believe the scriptures to be true and accurate (1 Thess. 2:13; Rom. 10:17).
5. Pray that God would bind Satan from blinding the eyes of the nonbeliever to the truth (Matt. 13:19; 2 Cor. 4:4).

6. Pray that the Holy Spirit would do his convicting work in the life of the nonbeliever (John 16:8-13).
7. Pray that God would send someone who would show the nonbeliever the way to faith in Christ (Matt. 9:37-38).
8. Pray that the nonbeliever would believe in Jesus Christ as his Lord and Savior (John 1:12; 5:24).
9. Pray that the nonbeliever would turn away from sin (Acts 17:30-31; 3:19).
10. Pray that the nonbeliever would confess Jesus Christ as Lord (Rom. 10:9-10).
11. Pray that the nonbeliever would yield everything in order to follow Jesus Christ (2 Cor. 5:15; Phil. 3:7-8).
12. Pray that the nonbeliever would take root and grow in Christ (Col. 2:6-7).
13. Pray that the nonbeliever would find satisfaction in nothing apart from God (Eccles. 1:2; 2:17).
14. Pray that the nonbeliever would seek to draw near to God (James 4:8).
15. Pray that the nonbeliever would not depend on his or her own works for salvation (Eph. 2:8-9).
16. Pray that the nonbeliever would see Jesus as the only option available for salvation (Acts 4:12).

Not only does prayer pave the way for personal evangelism, it is a prerequisite to mass evangelism. Christian history shows a pattern: first concentrated prayer, often prevailing prayer, and then revival.

The first Christian revival came as a result of ten days of united prayer. The 120 disciples were praying (Acts 1:14), and God added three thousand people to the church (Acts 2:41). The disciples began to pray again (Acts 2:42), and God "added daily" to the church (Acts 2:47). As the disciples continued to pray (Acts 3:1), five thousand more converts were added to the church (Acts 4:4). Continuing further in prayer (Acts 4:31-33), the scripture indicates that "multitudes" were continually being added to the church (Acts 5:14). By A.D. 100 it is estimated that somewhere in the vicinity of 5 percent of the Roman empire had become Christian. This could largely be attributed to the faithful praying of the early church, especially related to mass evangelism.

Led by the example of that first Christian revival, whenever revivals have occurred or spiritual awakenings have taken place, their beginnings have been found in the ministries of spirit-filled believers who were also mighty prayer warriors.

Often, God has responded to the prayers of believers by sending revival that not only revived the church but awakened society. Following are some examples of God-sent revival that began with prayer.

By A.D. 303, the number of believers in Asia Minor was equal to half the total population of the country, with the greatest period of growth between A.D. 260 and 303. This period, characterized by severe persecution, was likewise characterized by prayer.

In the twelfth century, a revival broke out among the Waldensians in Italy and the Alps. Peter Waldo, their first leader, was known as a man devoted to prayer.

By the year 1315, there were in Bohemia alone about 800,000 believers. By the time of the Reformation, they had four hundred local churches and the Bible translated in their language. Their leader, John Hus, was a man of prayer and organized the churches into prayer cells.

In the fourteenth century, John Wyclif, having opened again the Bible in his native England, founded the Society of the Lollards who went two-by-two throughout the land singing gospel verses. Wyclif was accustomed to spending hours in prayer.

In 1489, Savanarola was converted in Florence, Italy. So powerful were his sermons on lostness and Hell that the

When praying for revival evangelism, we should ask for:

- Workers for the harvest (Matt. 9:38)
- Cooperation among workers (1 Cor. 3:6)
- Open doors for the Gospel (Col. 4:2–3)
- Fruit that remains (John 15:16)
- Rapid spread of the Gospel (2 Thess. 3:1)
- A solid foundation of support for on-going evangelistic work (Rom. 10:14–15; Mark 16:15)

Turkish Muslim Sultan of that time requested the sermons be translated in Turkish so he could read them. Savanarola is regarded as the greatest Italian preacher of all time, sometimes drawing audiences of 10,000-to-20,000 people. His motto was As For Me, Prayer.

It is reported that Martin Luther prayed at length every day. A spy supposedly went to the inn where he was staying the night before he was to face his accusers in the law court in Worms on April 17, 1521. The spy noticed that Luther prayed all night long and was still on his knees at daybreak. When the spy returned to his superiors he declared, "Who can overcome such a man who prays thus."

Through prayer John Calvin made Geneva a city of God. It was his custom to study the Bible and prepare his lectures until 10:00 P.M. each evening. The following morning he would rise at 4:00 A.M. for meditation and prayer.

John Knox, the Scottish reformer who cried out "Give me Scotland or I die," spent nineteen months as a galley slave in South France for his preaching of the Gospel. During this time he prayed, "Lord, release me that I may return to Scotland to preach the Gospel to my compatriots there." Eventually, God returned him to Scotland to begin an evangelical, doctrinal, and spiritual revolution unparalleled in history. Queen Mary of Scotland testified concerning Knox, "I'd rather face an army of enemy soldiers than the prayers of John Knox."

In the 1630s, a revival broke out in the town of Shotts in Scotland. A young preacher named John Livingstone was asked to speak in the revival meeting the following day when the crowd was expected to gather. So terrified was this young man that he spent the evening in a wheat field on his face before the Lord in prayer. When he arrived to preach the next day, the record shows that five hundred souls were converted that day.

In the province of Ulster, in Northern Ireland, a group of pastors gathered to pray faithfully and to unite their ranks. Prior to this, they were not on speaking terms with each other. As their prayer meetings continued, they began to spend entire nights in prayer. Never did they consider a day or night long enough for the prayer meetings, nor was any room large enough to accommodate those who came to pray.

In 1735, Jonathan Edwards, the powerful preacher from Boston, spent an entire night in prayer. The following Sunday morning, he preached a sermon entitled, "Sinners in the Hands of an Angry God" based on Hebrews 10:31. Rather than being dynamic and forceful, Edwards read his sermon word for word with the manuscript held near his face because of his shortsightedness. Edwards himself was amazed when he happened to glance up from his notes to see people leaving the pews and clinging to the pillars of the church crying out, "Lord, have mercy on us." This meeting was part of the beginning of a great American awakening.

In July of 1745, David Brainerd went into the wilderness to preach the Gospel to the Indians. His body was already affected with the then deadly disease of tuberculosis. Brainerd spent long hours before the Lord pouring out his heart in intercessory prayer for the Indians. John Wesley declared to his followers, "Do you wish to have revival in your lives and in your ministry? Read the biography of David Brainerd." Brainerd was, according to one, a prophet of prayer for his generation.

In the seventeenth century, Richard Baxter was appointed as a minister in the Kidderminister Parish Church. Upon his arrival, he found only a small group of worshipers. Baxter began to pray until "the walls of his study became stained with his breath as he travailed in prayer." Then, as he began a program of pastoral evangelistic visitation and encouragement of every member, people began attending. Within five years, crowds were flocking to hear him preach in such large numbers that balcony after balcony was built in the church until there were a total of five.

The founder of the Society of Friends in the seventeenth century, George Fox, was a capable preacher, but above all he was mighty in prayer. One observer said of Fox, "I have never seen his like in prayer. His personality radiated the holiness, and majesty and love of God." It was the custom of George Fox to spend days alone in prayer, often hiding himself in a hollow trunk of a tree. Then he would return to speak God's word to the people with such effect that the results were awesome.

During the eighteenth century, John Wesley traveled as a missionary to America without having experienced the salvation of God. During a return journey by ship to England, he came in contact with some Moravian missionaries in whom he saw what was missing in his own life. As a result, Wesley came into a personal relationship with Jesus Christ through salvation, after which he spent a full hour each morning and another hour in the evening in prayer. He declared to himself, "There is no reason whatsoever that should prevent me from fulfilling this blessed practice."

Preceding the first Great Awakening in America in 1734, the people of God, whose hearts were broken over the deplorable conditions in America, began to pray earnestly to God for revival. Before and during the awakening, daily prayer meetings were initiated.

In 1742, William McCullough, pastor of a church in Canbuslang, Scotland, heard of the revival in England and America and longed to see similar revival in his own church. Following a revival meeting preached by the eloquent preacher, George Whitefield, revival continued in the Canbuslang church under Pastor McCullough until there was no room in the church auditorium for the crowds. Moving outside, McCullough then preached to open air crowds of between ten and twelve thousand people. McCullough prevailed in prayer, laboring in intercession for the souls of his listeners.

Prior to the second Great Awakening in America in 1792, Baptists, Congregationalists, Presbyterians, and others joined in regular prayer for another spiritual awakening. This concert of prayer again brought significant results.

The key to the success of the ministry of Charles Finney was twofold: his filling of the Holy Spirit and his life of prayer. It has been said that eighty-five percent of those who made professions of faith in Finney's revival meetings remained faithful to Christ and the church long after their public decisions. Finney led his converts into a life of prayer by personal example as well as by scriptural principles.

In 1839, a revival took place in Kilsyth, Scotland. The pastor of the church was W. C. Burns, a noted man of prayer. On one occasion he related to his congregation a story of the great revival that had taken place in the nearby town of Shotts more than two hundred years earlier. While he stood before his people praying to God for the Holy Spirit to descend, God sent revival and many of those present were saved. Visiting the nearby city of Dundee, Burns told the people what had happened in his own church, and again the Lord greatly blessed and gave many more souls. It is said that Burns spent days and nights before God in prayer.

After reading in *Second Evangelical Awakening in Britain*, J. Edwin Orr's accounts of the second Great Awakening in England during the 1860s, Stephen F. Olford concluded, "The two outstanding conditions for revival are unity and prayer."[2]

In regard to the revivals of 1904–1905, there is convincing evidence that prayer played an important role. This awakening was unique. Rather than springing forth from one locale and then spreading, it was a simultaneous worldwide movement of prayer. Significant were the prayers of teenagers for Evan Roberts of Wales.

The Shantung revivals in China may well be the most important event in the history of world missions. John Abernathy tells us, "In all the churches was held daily an early morning meeting for prayer and Bible study. . . . The revival came about as a result of earnest prayer by groups and individuals."[3] Concerning the involvement of Bertha Smith, Lewis Drummond writes:

> The missionaries of Shantung Province prevailed in prayer for revival in China, a country in dire need of a spiritual awakening. To Miss Bertha and her missionary partners in Shantung Province, the needs seemed particularly acute. So they devoted themselves to intercession for revival and they were not disappointed. Their prayers were heard. One glorious day God rent the heavens, and what is now called the Shantung Revival burst upon them. . . . In that inaugural year of revival, 1927, China experienced a genuine outpouring of the Holy Spirit that transformed multitudes.[4]

Concerning the Scottish revival in 1950, the noon prayer meetings gave way to prayer meetings and preaching services in the various evangelical churches on week nights, and in these churches there were numerous reported conversions.

The Asbury College revival in the early 1970s was one of several sparks that gave rise to a nationwide awakening among American youth. It began when a few concerned students met to pray for spiritual awakening. Likewise, the Canadian revivals in the 1970s came as a result of groups of Canadians praying for a revival.

Concerning the recent revivals in Korea during the 1980s and 1990s, Pastor Paul Cho indicated in regard to his own church revival, "We have seen the importance of developing and keeping a prayer life. If we stop praying, the revival will wane. If we continue praying, I believe all of Korea can be saved."[5] The Korean revivals have been marked by early morning prayer, all-night prayer meetings and prayer retreats. Reports are that whereas in 1900 there were no Protestant churches in Korea, today there are 36,000 churches (7,000 in Seoul alone). Furthermore, by latest estimates 26 percent of South Korea is Christian.

A recent awareness of God's powerful presence moved across the college and theological school campuses of America in the spring of 1995. With some involvement of local churches, the movement was primarily one among students marked by prayer, public confession of sin and calls for spiritual accountability. In the "Afterword" of the book *Revival,* Bill Bright says, "One prelude to the current revival movement has been the accelerated and unprecedented movements of prayers worldwide. God is hearing the prayers of His children around the world. Revival begins with prayer and results in evangelism."[6]

All of this supports statements by J. C. Ryle, who wrote:

I have read the lives of many eminent Christians who have been on the earth since the Bible days. Some of them, I see, were rich, and some poor. Some were learned, some unlearned. Some of them were Episcopalian, and some Christians of other denominations. Some were Calvinists, and some were Armenians. Some have loved to use liturgy, and some choose to use none. But one thing I see they all had in common, they all have been men of prayer.[7]

We must always be people of prayer and at the forefront of our praying, we must continue to ask God to send revival. Inspired by the revival prayer of Habakkuk, "O Lord, revive Your work in the midst of the years, in the midst of the years make it known" (Hab. 3:2), the Scottish Presbyterian minister and former physician William Mackay worded a prayer of his own. Set to music by a onetime choirboy at Westminster Abbey, John J. Husband, and popularized in the revival meetings of Ira Sankey, the hymn has been identified with revivalism since its writing more than 135 years ago:

> Revive us again; fill each heart with thy love;
> May each soul be rekindled with fire from above.
> Hallelujah! Thine the glory, Hallelujah! Amen;
> Hallelujah! Thine the glory, Revive us again.

If we have another significant spiritual awakening and revival in the world, it will come as God's people pray, and it will continue as God's people continue to pray. Prayer and evangelism are inseparably linked in the Word of God, in the human experience and, in Christian history. Behind all effective evangelism is regular, faithful prayer.

As the prayer-shaped disciple prays for the church and its evangelistic outreach, the natural result is to pray for world missions.

17. For World Missions:
Praying to the Ends of the Earth

Many people think of missions as ministry performed somewhere else, even to the remotest part of the earth. In reality, missions may be ministry performed where we live. Whether your concept of ministry is something which is performed nearby or far off, we must move beyond our normal prayer life to pray for "the ends of the earth" and those who live and work there. As author S. D. Gordon reminds us:

> Prayer puts us in direct dynamic touch with the world.... A man may go aside today and shut the door, and as really spend a half-hour of his life in India for God as though he were there in person. Surely you and I must get more half-hours for this secret service.[1]

The Bible instructs us to pray for missions. The psalmist records, "Ask of Me, and I will surely give the nations as Your inheritance, and the very ends of the earth as Your possession" (Ps. 2:8). The Apostle Paul instructs:

> First of all, then, I urge that entreaties and prayers, petitions and thanksgivings, be made on behalf of all men, . . .This is good and acceptable in the sight of God our Savior, who desires all men to be saved and to come to the knowledge of the truth. (1 Tim. 2:1, 3-4)

While there is no mention of prayer in the Great Commission as recorded in Acts (Acts 1:8), it is followed almost immediately with the words, "these all with one mind were continually devoting themselves to prayer" (Acts 1:14). The early believers went directly from receiving the commission to praying for their world. Within a matter of days, it was recorded that these disciples had "filled Jerusalem with [their] teaching" (Acts 5:28). The model is clear—from the Upper Room (with unity and prayer) to every room (with salvation and discipleship).

The Apostle Paul, the model of missionary enterprise, learned early the importance of the relationship between world missions and prayer. Immediately after his conversion, Paul began praying (Acts 9:10-11). Later, "they brought him [Paul] down to Caesarea and sent him away to Tarsus" (Acts 9:30). No reference to Paul is made for seven-to-ten years. There were no missionary journeys taken. There were no converts won. There were no new churches started. What was Paul doing during this time? It is obvious from the earlier reference that he was praying. At the end of the seven-to-ten years God said to Ananias, "Inquire at the house of Judas for a man from Tarsus named Saul, for behold he is praying" (Acts 9:11). We may well assume that Paul had been praying consistently during the years of silence. Then when the church at Antioch was ready to commission Paul and Barnabas for missionary service, they sent them away in prayer (Acts 13:3).

In addition to the Biblical base Christian history likewise makes the connection between prayer and missions. Every fresh burst of missionary energy has been preceded by believing prayer. Charles Spurgeon prayed, "Lord, give me a dozen importunate pleaders and lovers of souls, and by Thy grace I will shake London from end to end." Many a world shaking has begun among praying believers.

In the seventeenth century, Justinian Welz became a prophetic voice for world missions. Few paid any attention to his utterances and his writings until later in the next century. In 1723 Robert Millar, a Presbyterian minister, wrote *A History of the Propagation of Christianity and the Overthrow of Paganism*, in which he advocated intercession as the primary means of converting "the heathen." In the summer of 1727, the Moravian Brethren held a "round-the-clock prayer watch" seven days per week, which continued for approximately one hundred years. This was the beginning of the modern missionary movement as young men out of the Moravian faith in response to the intercessory prayer of other Moravians answered God's call to begin missionary work in the Virgin Islands. In 1732, missionaries were sent to the slaves on the island of St. Thomas.

In 1747, Christians in Boston entered into a seven-year "concert of prayer" for missionary work. The following year Jonathan Edwards responded with a call for all believers to engage in intercessory prayer for the spread of the Gospel throughout the earth. In 1783, a call went to all Baptists to set aside the first Monday of each month for united intercessory prayer for "the heathen of the world." In 1792, William Carey sailed for India under the Baptist Missionary Society.

In 1806, missionaries crossed the Atlantic and landed at Williams College in Williamstown, Massachusetts. There a group of students, led by Samuel J. Mills, covenanted to pray together and study the Bible. On a Wednesday afternoon, in a thunderstorm and under a haystack for protection, the group committed themselves to missions to the ends of the earth. They signed a pledge to be America's first foreign missionaries; thus began the Student Volunteer Missions Movement—the beginning of missionary activity from within the United States.

Later in the nineteenth century, Hudson Taylor of the China Inland Mission began his fifty years of service during which it was said the sun never rose in China without finding Hudson Taylor on his knees. He was the father of modern missions.

These are but a few samples of the relationship between prayer and world missionary activity. A study of mission history reveals that behind every outburst of real missions in the life of the church, we find those who have prayed until the Spirit of God has come upon them; then in the Spirit's power have gone out to witness the mighty acts of God. In every case the new movement to world mission parallels the waiting, praying group of disciples in the upper room at Pentecost.

Not only does the Bible call us to pray for missions (and Christian history demonstrates that relationship), but the current scene also challenges us to pray for missionary activity. It is estimated that up to three-fourths of the world are non-Christians and the most rapid growth in the world is in "third-world countries" where Christian witness is not strong. Of the world's population:

- 26 percent are atheists
- 13 percent are Hindus
- 8 percent are Buddhists
- 17 percent are Muslims
- 33 percent are Christians (18 percent of these are Roman Catholic, leaving 15 percent as non-Catholic evangelicals).

It is estimated that in this century no more than three hundred thousand persons have been converted out of Islam, and that only about 1 percent of the Christians in India have been converted out of Hinduism. Converts out of Buddhism number only a few thousand. The majority of the non-Christians in the world can only be reached by cross-cultural missionary effort. The current scene calls us to pray for missionary endeavor.

What should you do about prayer and world missions? First, you should be informed about missionary opportunities and missionary activity. Read missionary journals and magazines. Listen to missionaries on every possible occasion. When missionaries have newsletters, get on their mailing lists so you can stay up-to-date with their activity. Modern communication methods such as e-mail make instant prayer requests possible. Finally, participate in mission action groups sponsored by local churches and in some cases para-church organizations.

Once informed about missions, pray about them specifically. While not everyone can go, every believer can pray. Even if you travel to some distant place, you have only gone to one place; whereas through prayer you can cover the world.

Some of the missions-related needs for which we should pray include:

- Spiritual depth which is lacking in many counties of the world
- Male leadership of which there is a lack in all sending agencies and in every country of the world
- A spirit of optimism among missionaries since believers represent a small minority in many countries
- Pure doctrine as it is always challenged by the prevailing philosophies and superstitions and religious trends of the country
- Healthy working relationships among missionaries
- Governmental cooperation and support
- Genuine spiritual revival which is needed in almost every country of the world
- Effective and challenging strategies in days of rapid change
- Wise use of resources, both human and material
- Missionaries themselves—for their health, their language adjustment, their protection, their mental adjustment, their emotions, their culture shock, their personal relationships, their families both present and away, and their spiritual growth
- Children of missionaries—some are removed from their parents, whether in boarding school, back in the U.S. in college, or in some other way. One of the best ministries you can perform for missionaries is to pray for MKs (Missionary's Kids—see sidebar, next page)

- Scripture translation and distribution into all languages and into all parts of the world (The Global Evangelization Database lists 11,874 ethnolinguistic groups and 24,000 languages in the world. Conservative estimates say we now have entire Bibles in 273 languages, New Testaments in 472 languages. There are 3,418 language groups with no portion of scripture available in their language.)
- Allow a current copy of the newspaper to call your attention to world events which might affect missionary endeavors
- In front of a current world map, allow God to call attention to certain countries where intercession is needed
- When awakened during the night—pray for something that is happening on the other side of the world where it is daylight. Some must keep the night watches

---

How can you pray effectively for MKs?

- Pray for their coping with homesickness —for parents, for U.S. culture, for friends left behind, and for church.
- Pray for relationships—with other MKs, with missionaries, with nationals, with extended families, and with friends.
- Pray for their spiritual condition—for salvation, for rededication, for calling from God, for daily walk with God, and for resistance to sin.
- Pray for influences on their life—for good friends, good teachers, and good extended family.
- Pray for emotions—often difficult to express due to changes in culture, language, and relationships .

I correspond with more than one hundred former students who presently serve in cross-cultural settings. Their names, when attached to a global map, reach around the world. I pray regularly for them in my daylight hours. Realizing that the sun never sets on my former students, I also find myself awakened in the night with their names on my mind. It is God's plan that a guard of prayer shall be set up by the church all day and all night (Ps. 63:6; Isa. 50:4). The poet Marianne Farminham expressed the need for praying for those far away when their names come to our minds:

I cannot tell why there should come to me
    A thought of someone miles and miles away!
In swift insistence on the Memory,
    Unless a need there be that I should pray.

Too hurried oft are we to spare the thought,
    For days together, of some friends away:
Perhaps God does it for us, and we ought
    To read His signal as a call to pray.

Perhaps, just then, my friend has fiercer fight,
    And more appalling weakness and decay
Of courage, darkness, some lost sense of right;
    And so, in case he needs my prayer, I pray.

Friend, do the same for me. If I intrude
    Unasked upon you, on some crowded day,
Give me a moment's prayer as interlude;
    Be very sure I need it, therefore, pray.

In addition to learning and praying specifically about world missions, you could allow prayer to guide you into direct participation. Ask God what you should give financially. Another possibility is a God-called life commitment to mission enterprises. Where life commitments and career changes are not in order, you can still be involved on a short-term basis through mission-sending agencies, both church and para-church related. In my travels, I find an increasing number of short-term personnel filling crucial roles on mission fields. Some stay a few weeks, others months, some for a year or more.

An individual or a family might well adopt a particular mission field, people group, or specific missionary and participate in ministry through prayer, giving, and even short-term support visits. Churches are beginning to sponsor prayer journeys into mission fields. On one agency's recent international short-term needs list, I estimated one-third of the requests were for prayer teams. I presently have on my desk requests from six nations for student prayer teams for the upcoming summer. The means of direct involvement are open and endless for those who pray.

The relationship between prayer and world missions cannot be over-emphasized. It is true that the evangelization of the world waits first of all upon a revival of prayer. Deeper than the need for missionaries—deeper far than the need for finances—is the need for prevailing worldwide prayer.

We all could learn from the example of Presbyterian missionary John "Praying" Hyde, who served in India during the nineteenth century. Hyde was slow of speech and hard of hearing, but he realized that the Mohammedan priests were praying at 5:00 A.M. each day. Impressed by this, Hyde began to pray from 4:00 A.M. to 5:00 A.M. daily for "one soul per day or I die." At the end of the first year, there were over four hundred Christian converts as a result of the ministry of John Hyde. Hyde then adjusted his prayer to "two souls per day or I die." At the end of the second year there were over eight hundred persons who had become Christians. Further challenged, Hyde prayed, "Four souls a day or I die." It was during that year that Hyde died of a "displaced heart," meaning that the heart had moved within his chest. He had lived the last months of his life under terrific stress. It was John Hyde who said, "I'd rather burn out than rust out."[2]

Author Leonard Ravenhill shares another example of intercessory prayer out of the life of John Hyde:

Dr. J. Wilbur Chapman was once preaching in Hereford, England. For days there was a signal absence of power and conviction of sin. "But when John Hyde came there, God came to town," said Wilbur Chapman. God and Hyde walked together. (Amazing condescension of God!) As a result, when Chapman made the appeal on the first night after Hyde was in that town, fifty men came to Christ. Chapman begged Hyde, "Pray for me." Into a room these two men went; Hyde turned the key in the door, turned his face up to God, then turned the fountains of his great heart open. Chapman adds, "I felt the hot tears running down my face. I knew I was with God. With upturned face, down which the tears were streaming, John Hyde said two words: 'Oh God!' For five minutes at least, he was still again, and then when he knew he was talking with God, his arm went around my shoulder, and there came up from the depth of his heart such petitions for men as I had never before heard. I rose from my knees to know what real prayer was."

Down to his feeblest days, Hyde prayed. Hear him in a letter to his sister:"I am still in bed or in a wheel chair, getting a fine rest and doing a lot of the ministry of intercession." In the Lord's book of remembrance we shall see the mighty results of the prayer ministry that this lover of men's souls exercised.[3]

Former Southern Baptist missionary to China, Bertha Smith, set the following example:

Bertha wanted everyone saved. The Lord laid on her heart twenty young people about her own age who did not know Christ. She prayed for them, daily naming each one before the Lord. Eighteen of those were saved that same summer. The nineteenth came to Christ some years later. The twentieth had moved away and Bertha lost contact.[4]

Often, we can accomplish more for the salvation of persons by praying for them than we can by any other way.

Finally, the example of Art Wiens and Jim Elliot challenges us all:

Art Wiens, for long years a missionary in central Italy, and Jim Elliott, well-known Auca Indian martyr, formed a group of Wheaton College students to pray for missions. There were one thousand five hundred students on campus in 1947. Why not ask God to send one thousand of them to the mission field? Confidently they prayed. Art besought God for every student, following the student directory. Today Wiens' tattered prayer diary, kept since college days, includes 535 missionaries scattered throughout the world, from that period, whom Art prays for regularly by name! Only the dedicated effort of those years can explain the numbers of effective workers around the world today from Wheaton College, in that important period.[5]

> Away in foreign fields, they wondered how
>   Their simple word had power—
> At home, some Christians, two or three, had met
>   To pray an hour.
> We are always wondering—wondering how,
>   Because we do not see
> Someone—Perhaps unknown and far away—
>   On bended knee.[6]

As the prayer-shaped disciple becomes increasingly and effectively involved in praying for the world, eventually Satan gets distressed and goes on the attack. Then the pray-er becomes a prayer warrior as spiritual warfare commences.

18. Into Spiritual Warfare:
Praying as to War

No sooner did the early church begin to carry out their Lord's Great Commission than it became involved in spiritual warfare. In Acts, Luke records various encounters between the church and Satan. The first one is in Acts 5 where Satan attacked the church from within through a prominent church family, Ananias and Sapphira. God counter-attacked with judgment of the disobedient believers and drove back the forces of Satan. In Acts 8, God moved to separate the church in Jerusalem from its Jewish comfort zone through heavy persecution. Even more dramatic warfare is observed in Acts 13 when Satan's representative was humiliated, defeated, and blinded through the ministry of Paul. In Acts 16, warfare was fought over the demonized slave girl of Philippi. Finally, in Acts 19, warfare was waged between the Spirit of God and the evil spirits associated with some Jewish exorcists in Ephesus. These and other encounters repeatedly called the early church to prayer.

In a more modern application, I have encountered spiritual warfare most heavily in evangelism (both personal and mass evangelism), pre-evangelism that seriously leads to direct evangelism, and prevailing prayer, especially for non-Christians. Prayer is communication with the Commander-in-Chief. Just like warfare, Satan tries to weaken the offense (evangelism) and cut off the communication (prayer). Thus there is a:

> Strong and powerful relationship between putting on the armor of God and praying. These two things belong together; in fact, one grows out of the other. It is not enough to put on the armor of God—you must also pray. It is not enough to pray—you must have also put on the armor of God.[1]

When I think of spiritual warfare, I liken it to the commands of the Bible Sword Drills of my childhood and teenage years: "Sword Drills" were contests to see who could find a specified scripture verse the fastest. Our leaders cued us with the commands, "Attention! Draw Swords! Charge!"

Attention! (Eph. 6:10–13). Coming to attention is related to prayer in Luke: "But keep on the alert at all times, praying that you may have strength to escape all these things that are about to take place, and to stand before the Son of Man" (Luke 21:36).

First, let's give attention to our empowering. The psalmist says, "Seek the Lord and His strength; Seek His face continually" (Ps. 105:4), and "On the day I called, You answered me; You made me bold with strength in my soul" (Ps. 138:3). Why do we need empowering? We are camped in enemy territory. We are strangers and sojourners in this land. Paul speaks of power as being active, like the weight lifter lifting weights. He also speaks of might, which is passive power demonstrated by the same weight lifter wearing a muscle T-shirt, while not lifting weights. Power is not being exercised but it is evident.

Second, as we give attention to our equipping, Martyn Lloyd-Jones helps us:

> Praying in the spirit is something we have to do, and to keep on doing, in connection with the use of the whole armor, and indeed with the whole of our position as Christians in conflict with the world and the flesh and the devil . . . The armor which is provided

for us by God cannot be used except in fellowship and communion with God.[2]

As Paul reminds us, "The weapons of our warfare are not of the flesh, but divinely powerful " (2 Cor. 10:4).

Jesus wants to equip us: "If you then, being evil, know how to give good gifts to your children, how much more will your heavenly Father give the Holy Spirit to those who ask Him?" (Luke 11:13). For two years Paul was chained to Roman soldiers, observing their armor and comparing it to spiritual warfare. He then described it in detail. We now have the responsibility to pick up the armor. Armor not picked up is worthless. The following report from the Deputy Chief of the Los Angeles Police Department illustrates the value of putting on our armor in the midst of conflict:

The sun was just coming up. The motorcycle officer moved smoothly through the quiet Los Angeles suburb on his way in to work. As he neared an intersection, a red pickup truck sped past without even slowing for the stop sign. The officer turned on his flashing lights and radioed the station that he was in pursuit of the red vehicle.

As his unit pulled up behind the slowing truck, the officer was thinking, "This fellow is probably late for work." Unknown to the officer, the driver of the pickup had just robbed an all night grocery store. On the seat beside the driver was the paper bag with the money and the gun he had used. The driver was thinking, "The cops know already." He was scared. He rested his hand on the gun.

The truck pulled to the side of the roadway and stopped. The officer parked his motorcycle and approached the driver's side of the pickup. He was relaxed, "Good morning sir. May I see your ... " He didn't even get to finish his sentence. The driver stuck his arm out of the truck and fired his weapon. The barrel of the gun was only two inches away from the officer. The bullet hit the officer in the center of his chest. He was knocked to the ground seven feet away.

For a few moments, all was quiet. Then, to the horror of the gunman, the officer slowly stood to his feet. The driver couldn't believe it, "This guy must be Superman." In shock, the policeman slowly began to brush the dirt from his uniform. After two or three seconds, the officer regained his wits, pulled his service revolver, and fired two rounds into the side of the truck. The first round went through the open window and destroyed the windshield. The second round went through the side of the door and ripped into the driver's left leg. "Don't shoot," screamed the terrified robber, throwing the gun and the bag of money out of the window.

The officer's life had been spared because he was wearing a bulletproof vest. Vests are incredibly strong even though they are only about three-eighths of an inch thick. They are made of dozens of layers of an extremely tough fabric—Kevlar.

A few months later another officer, Ray Hicks, and his partner went to serve a search warrant on a well-known drug dealer in the city of Inglewood. As his partner knocked, Hicks yelled out "Police!" and started to kick down the door. From inside the shabby apartment, four slugs were fired through the door. One found its mark. The impact was almost exactly where the motorcycle officer had been hit only a few weeks before—squarely in the center of the chest.

Later his partner recalled that Hicks said quietly, "I'm hit," and slowly sank to the floor. The coroner reported that the policeman probably lived less than a minute. The bullet had ruptured an artery; blood to the brain had been stopped instantly.

Police officer Ray Hicks was 27 years old. He left a wife, three children, and a bullet proof vest in the trunk of his car parked 30 feet from where he fell.

Every police officer in Los Angeles believes in bullet proof vests. They work! I doubt you could find a policeman anywhere who doesn't believe vests save lives.

But that is not enough. An officer must do more than believe in vests. He must take his belief to the point of personal commitment. He must be willing to wear the vest, and wear it at all times. Even when it is hot. Even when it is uncomfortable.[3]

Finally we focus on the enemy. Again, the psalmist says, "Then my enemies will turn back in the day when I call; this I know, that God is for me" (Ps. 56:9). This was hand-to-hand combat which involved not four classes of demons but four ways of seeing one enemy (v. 12). The battlefield where the enemy is encountered is in "high places"—not geographical, but supernatural (v. 12). Satan fears little on earth as much as prayer. He doesn't know how to cope with it, so he concentrates on three strategies: keeping believers from prayer, distracting believers' attention in prayer, and hindering the success of prayer, thus discouraging the believer before the answer comes.

However, Satan is limited in authority. Only God is sovereign. Satan could not touch Job (Job 1–2) or Peter (Luke 22:31). Satan is limited in knowledge. Only God is omniscient. Satan may know more than you, but never more than God. Satan is limited in power. Only God is omnipotent. Satan has great power but not more than God (1 John 4:4; 2 Kings 6:16). Satan is limited in presence. Only God is omnipresent. Satan cannot be everywhere at once. He can only be in one place at a time. Thus, he has to depend on his demons and angels. They have even less authority, knowledge, and power than Satan.

Satan is a defeated foe. Repeatedly the Bible assures us of victory:

In all these things we overwhelmingly conquer through Him who loved us. (Rom. 8:37)

When He had disarmed the rulers and authorities, He made a public display of them, having triumphed over them through Him. (Col. 2:15)

Submit therefore to God. Resist the devil and he will flee from you. (James 4:7)

[Jesus Christ], who is at the right hand of God, having gone into heaven, after angels and authorities and powers had been subjected to Him. (1 Pet. 3:22)

Then I heard a loud voice in heaven, saying, "Now the salvation, and the power, and the kingdom of our God and the authority of His Christ have come, for the accuser of our brethren has been thrown down, he who accuses them before our God day and night. And they overcame him because of the blood of the Lamb and because of the word of their testimony, and they did not love their life even when faced with death." (Rev. 12:10–11).

Through our prayers we are planting the blood-stained flag of our King in another kingdom's battlefield. Slowly the kingdoms of this world are becoming God's.

Draw Swords! We must prepare both defensively and offensively. The psalmist says, "Incline Your ear to me, . . . for You are my rock and my fortress [defense]; for Your name's sake You will lead me and guide me" (Ps. 31:2–3).

Paul lists the pieces of *defensive* armor in Ephesians 6:14–17. There is the Belt of Truth (v. 14). The psalmist writes concerning truth, "Not to us, O Lord, not to us, but to Your name give glory. Because of Your lovingkindness, because of Your truth" (Ps. 115:1); "The Lord is near to all who call upon Him, to all who call upon Him in truth" (Ps. 145:18). This was a leather belt that held everything else together, as well as gave support for the back.

There was the Breastplate of Righteousness (v. 14). Concerning righteousness, the Bible says, "Then he will pray to God, and He will accept him, that he may see His face with joy, and He may restore His righteousness to man" (Job 33:26). "Answer me when I call, O God of my righteousness" (Ps. 4:1). "The effective prayer of a righteous man can accomplish much" (James 5:16). This piece of armor protected vital organs (heart and emotions). The psalmist said, "I have been young, and now I am old, yet I have not seen the righteous forsaken" (Ps. 37:25). We sometimes sing, "Dressed in his righteousness alone" as an expression of putting on this piece of armor.

Added to the belt and the breastplate were the Shoes of the Gospel of Peace (v. 15). Concerning peace, Jeremiah writes, "Seek the peace of the city where I have caused you to be carried away captive, and pray to the Lord for it; for in its peace you will have peace" (Jer. 29:7 NKJV). In Deuteronomy 29:5, the shoes never wore out in the wilderness. Likewise, the Gospel will never wear out. These were hob-nail sandals which gave the soldiers good traction, enabling them to relax without falling.

Another piece of defensive armor was the Shield of Faith (v. 16). James writes about faith, "If any of you lacks wisdom, let him ask of God, who gives to all men generously and without reproach, and it will be given to him. But he must ask in faith without any doubting" (James 1:5–6). This was not a small shield for the word also means "door." The enemy darts or arrows were dipped in pitch and set afire. The shield, made of bronze and oxide, gave protection from these fiery darts. A shield that size may have looked foolish to the enemy. Faith often looks foolish to those who have none.

The final piece of defensive armor was the Helmet of Salvation (v. 17). The psalmist writes of salvation, "O Lord, the God of my salvation, I have cried out by day and in the night before You" (Ps. 88:1). This piece we are to "take" as a gift for it protects the head or mind (Job 2:6; Rom. 12:2). In Isaiah 59:17, we are told the Lord wears this piece of armor.

Not only must we put on *defensive* armor, we must draw our *offensive* armor—the Sword of the Spirit (v. 17). The early spiritual warriors said, "We will devote ourselves to prayer and to the ministry of the word" (Acts 6:4). Some contend that all armor for spiritual warfare is defensive. To this Walter Wink responds, "It is humorous to watch the statement bob from scholar to scholar that the weapons here are all 'defensive.' The Pentagon says the same about nuclear missiles."[4] Jesus drew this sword in the midst of his temptation (Matt. 4:1-11) by quoting Deuteronomy 8:3 and 6:16 and on the cross by quoting from Psalm 22:1 and 31:5. Peter Wagner, who has made an exhaustive study of spiritual warfare in recent years, observes, "Instead of going about His business and allowing Satan to choose the time and place of attack, Jesus took the initiative and went on the offensive immediately after His baptism."[5] In fact, the place chosen by Jesus for his preparation for the battle was the wilderness. The Greek word for wilderness is *eremos*, meaning "a place of deadly danger and of demonic powers." The gates of hell cannot withstand the offensive attack of Jesus even though gates are defensive weapons.

Note also there was no armor for the back. It was not needed for there was to be no retreating by the forces of God.

Writing concerning this passage in Ephesians, Mark Bubeck notes:

A believer who brings to grasp the tremendous power of his spiritual weaponry through understanding passages like this will find a new joy in prayer. Prayer is the chief means by which our faith expresses itself. Prayer is the chief means by which we employ and appropriate the victory which is ours over all principalities and powers. The mighty resources in prayer remain yet to be tapped in most believers' lives.[6]

The third command from Bible Sword Drills is *Charge!* (Eph. 6:18-20). We are to charge first of all with prayer (v. 18). At this point especially, warfare and prayer are inseparable. Warfare without the practice of prayer is powerless; prayer that does not anticipate spiritual warfare is foolish. Prayer here is the more inclusive word meaning the whole act of worship, while supplication is the more narrow word meaning petition.

Particularly you should pray for Christian leaders. They will, as Paul did, need the prayer support of intercessors in the midst of the conflict. Effective leaders, always come under attack, especially immediately after a spiritual victory. They will need help, for no leader possesses enough within himself or herself to succeed in the battle alone. The weaknesses of the leaders need to be matched with the strengths of the intercessors. Then, when effective, spiritual leaders will motivate and encourage others in the battle. As was the case with Paul in spiritual warfare, such was the case with Joshua in physical warfare. The principles are the same:

> Then Amalek came and fought against Israel at Rephidim. So Moses said to Joshua, "Choose men for us and go out, fight against Amalek. Tomorrow I will station myself on the top of the hill with the staff of God in my hand." Joshua did as Moses told him, and fought against Amalek; and Moses, Aaron, and Hur went up to the top of the hill. So it came about when Moses held his hand up, that Israel prevailed, and when he let his hand down, Amalek prevailed. But Moses' hands were heavy. Then they took a stone and put it under him, and he sat on it; and Aaron and Hur supported his hands, one on one side and one on the other. Thus his hands were steady until the sun set. So Joshua overwhelmed Amalek and his people with the edge of the sword. (Exod. 17:8-13)

As you pray in the midst of spiritual warfare, the intensity increases. In their book *Power House: A Step-By-Step Guide to Building a Church that Prays*, Glen Martin and Dian Ginter identify six levels of prayer:

Level 1: *Introduction,* when a believer first starts to realize that it is possible to personally talk to God about those things of concern.

Level 2: *Initiation,* where a believer reaches beyond self and family to broaden praying to include a wider scope of requests.

Level 3: *Imitation,* where a believer becomes more aware of how others are praying.

Level 4: *Intercession,* where a believer finds himself or herself with a growing burden to intercede.

Level 5: *Investigation,* where a believer finds their faith increasing to believe God can and will do what is requested in prayer.

Level 6: *Invasion,* where a believer enters into spiritual warfare.[7]

We don't know whether prayer is the first point or a part of every point in the strategy, but we do know what happens when prayer has no part in it. Above all else, we are to stay in contact with the Commander-in-Chief, God, since the battle is not ours. The biblical promise is strong: "Do not fear or be dismayed because of this great multitude, for the battle is not yours but God's" (2 Chron. 20:15).

Not only are we to charge with prayer, we are also to charge with proclamation (vv. 19–20). We need not expect an easy way out, but we may expect a strength not our own to do the undoable, to bear the unbearable, and to face the unfaceable. What we can expect is God's help in proclaiming the Gospel, and through God's help, victory is inevitable. We witness this with Peter, John, and "their company" in Acts 4:13, 29, and 31. In Philippians 1:20 Paul prays for "utterance," verbalizing the faith. He saw himself as an ambassador, one who represents a King in another kingdom.

The greater our God-given responsibilities, the more time we need with God to seek guidance, empowerment, and protection. Prayer takes time, but it also makes time by multiplying the effectiveness of the believer's proclamation. So, we must heed the words of George Duffield, Jr.:

Stand up, stand up for Jesus,
Stand in His strength alone;
The arm of flesh will fail you,
Ye dare not trust your own.

Put on the gospel armor,
Each piece put on with prayer;
Where duty calls or danger,
Be never wanting there.

Conclusion

We have now considered what it means to be a prayer-shaped disciple. Having done so, it is time to think about moving from prayer to the other activities of the Christian life before we say a final "Amen."

In my early post-seminary-degree days, I was in campus ministry at Pan American University (now The University of Texas at Pan American) located on the Mexican border in south Texas. I had taken a group of students to a rustic mountain camp southwest of Mexico City for a joint retreat with students from the National University of Mexico. Upon arrival, we were warned not to go outside of the camp toward the mountains due to the presence of wild animals there. Shortly after the evening session, some students came to my cabin to inform me that "Jimmy was missing." Jimmy was an outdoors type as well as somewhat of a loner. Word of his absence had spread quickly among the students. When I got to the Dining Hall where the others had gathered, I found them discussing what to do. The solutions were varied, but no one really had a good answer. Jimmy was missing. Someone had seen him walking toward the mountains. It was dark and getting cool. If Jimmy did not return soon, something had to be done. Suddenly, one of the more spiritual students suggested that what we really needed to do was "pray about it" and began to give instructions to form a prayer circle. Eric, another student, had not been a Christian very long and not only did he not understand much about prayer, but he still maintained a lot of his pre-Christian lifestyle and language. He watched as everyone moved about for a few seconds before his old nature kicked in. Then, in one loud, profane, yet thought-provoking outburst, Eric said, "Pray, hell! Let's go get Jimmy!"

As important as prayer is and as high a priority as it occupies in the Christian life, there comes a time to get off our knees and on our feet, to get out of the prayer-room and into the arena. There comes a time to stop praying and "go get Jimmy." (By the way, we prayed first, then we went looking for Jimmy.) A. J. Gordon said, "You can do more than pray after you have prayed, but you cannot do more than pray until you have prayed." We didn't find Jimmy that night. The next morning as we were eating breakfast he walked into camp. He had lost his way and spent the night in the mountains. Other than a touch of frostbite, he was fine, having provided a significant prayer lesson for a group of university students and one future seminary professor.

Now, the concluding Amen.

We have affirmed that prayer is two-way communication. We have explored the idea that a prayer-shaped disciple should pray *with*, *through*, and *beyond*. We have concluded that there is much to be done through and in addition to prayer. So, to the work—the work of prayer, a glorious, yet often misunderstood work. Walker of Tinnevelly, after years of missionary service, resigned from some of his responsibilities in order to devote more time to prayer. The local newspaper reported that Rev. T. Walker used to be a hard worker but now had retired to pray. In his pamphlet on prayer, Walker wrote:

> Better, far better, do less work, if need be, that we may pray more; because work done by the rushing torrent of human energy will not save a single soul; whereas work done in vital and unbroken contact with the living God will tell for all eternity.[1]

One of my favorite Bible characters is Epaphras. He is only mentioned once in Scripture (Col. 4:12). All we know about Epaphras is that he was one of the believers in Colosse who was known for "laboring earnestly . . . in his prayers." Why was Epaphras not better known? Because he chose the often overlooked, low-profile work of prayer. Laboring in near obscurity, he performed the invaluable ministry of intercession. Others were more visible and less effective. Whether visible or invisible, it's time to pray.

So we conclude with a formula, a prayer, and an Amen. First, the formula:

- The more time you spend with God, the more your God-given responsibilities and the less your human busy work.
- The less time you spend with God, the less your God-given responsibilities and the more your human busy work.
- Spend little time with God and you will grow weary in well doing.
- Spend much time with God and you will find seasons of refreshing for your soul.

My closing prayer is in the words of Charles Wesley's 1740 hymn "Talk With Us, Lord," which was addressed to God, "Who by his power within us is able to do infinitely more than we ever dare to ask or imagine—to him be glory in the Church and in Christ Jesus for ever and ever, Amen" (Eph. 3:20–21, Phillips).

> Talk with us Lord, Thyself reveal,
> While here o'er earth we rove;
> Speak to our hearts, and let us feel
> The kindling of Thy love.
>
> With Thee conversing, we forget
> All time and toil and care;
> Labor is rest, and pain is sweet,
> If Thou, My God, art here.
>
> Thou callest me to seek Thy face,
> 'Tis all I wish to seek;

> To hear the whispers of Thy grace,
> And hear Thee in me speak.
>
> Let this my every hour employ,
> Till I Thy glory see
> Enter into my Master's joy,
> And find my heav'n in Thee.

Finally, the Amen. The word "Amen" means to support, to be firm, true, reliable. It is an exclamation by which we affirm that we are ready to bear the consequences of what has been communicated. Someday the last prayer will be prayed and the kneeling bench of earthly prayer will become the podium of eternal praise. Until then, be ever found praying and "let the Amen sound from his people again." In the words of Isaac Watts:

> Call upon God, adore, confess,
> Petition, plead, and then declare.
> You are the Lord's, give thanks and bless,
> And let Amen confirm the prayer.

Endnotes

Part One: The Prayer-Shaped Disciple Prays *With*

1. William J. Reynolds, *Companion to Baptist Hymnal* (Nashville: Broadman Press, 1976), p. 96.

1. Heavenly Prayer Partners: Connecting with Heaven

1. Dick Eastman and Jack Hayford, *Living and Praying in Jesus Name* (Wheaton: Tyndale House Publishers, Inc., 1988), p. 9.
2. Alexander Maclaren, "A Pattern of Prayer." In *Classic Sermons on Prayer*, ed., Warren Wiersbe (Grand Rapids: Kregel Publications, 1987), p. 114.
3. George A. Buttrick, *The Power of Prayer Today* (Waco: Word Books, 1970), p. 33.
4. Carolyn Gilman, "And He's Ever Interceding" (Nashville: John T. Benson Publishing Company, 1980)
5. Paul Y. Cho, *Prayer: Key to Revival* (Waco: Word Books, 1970), p. 33.

6. Wesley Duewel, *Touch the World Through Prayer* (Grand Rapids: Francis Asbury Press, 1986), pp.76–86.

7. "Missionaries Credit Prayer with Saving Their Lives," *Baptist Messenger* (September 2, 1993): 5.

8. J. I. Packer, *Keeping in Step with the Spirit* (Old Tappan, N.J.: Fleming H. Revell, 1984), pp.79–80.

9. R. A. Torrey, *Power of Prayer* (Grand Rapids: Zondervan Press, 1982), p. 75.

10. "Angels", *SBC Life* (Summer 1993): 12.

11. Geron Davis, Ignatius Meimaris, "Holy Ground," Nashville: Meadowgreen Group, 1983).

2. Earthly Prayer Partners: Where Two or Three Are Gathered

1. James H. McConkley, "The Practice of Prayer," *Mighty Prevailing Prayer*, comp. A. Sims (Grand Rapids: Zondervan Publishing House, n.d.): 13.

2. Charles Francis Whitson, *Pray: A Study of Distinctive Christian Praying* (Grand Rapids: Wm. B. Eerdmans Publishing Co., 1972), p. 118.

3. Mary White, "Dear God, Please Make My Nostrils Work," *Discipleship Journal*, issue 53, (1989): 62. See also "Altering the Family Altar," *Focal Point*, Vol. 7, No. 4 Oct.-Dec. (Englewood, Co.: Denver Seminary, 1987): 5.

4. Robert E. Coleman, *Introducing the Prayer Cell* (Huntingdon Valley, Pa: Christian Outreach, 1960), p. 6.

5. W. E. Sangster, *How to Form a Prayer Cell*, Westminster Pamphlet, no. 10 (London: E.P. Worth, 1958), p. 3.

6. Dietrich Bonhoeffer, *Life Together*, trans. by J. W. Doberstein (New York: Harper and Row Publishers, 1954), p. 63.

3. Awareness of God's Responses: Listen up

1. R. W. Goetsch, *Power through Prayer* (St. Louis: Concordia Publishing House, 1959), p. 38.

2. Charles G. Finney, *Prevailing Prayer* (Grand Rapids: Kregel Publication, 1965), p. 41.

3. Reported by various sources as being written by an unknown Confederate soldier and other sources as being written by Col. R. H. Fitzhugh.

4. Basic Ingredients: ACTing Up

1. George A. Buttrick, *The Power of Prayer Today* (Waco: Word Books, 1970), p. 52.
2. Paul E. Billheimer, *Destined for the Throne* (Fort Washington, Pa: Christian Literature Crusade, 1975), p. 118.
3. Wesley L. Duewel, *Touch the World Through Prayer* (Grand Rapids: Francis Asbury Press, 1986), p. 143.
4. Timothy Dudley-Smith, *Songs of Deliverance* (Carol Stream, Ill.: Hope Publishing Company, 1988), p. 29.
5. Adapted from "How to Confess to Your Mate," *Spirit of Revival*, Buchanan, Mich. (Vol. 25, Number 2): 18.
6. For further information read the pamphlet, *Counsel on Open Confession* by Jim Elliff (North Little Rock: Christian Communicators Worldwide, Inc., 1995).

5. Privacy: Where One Is Gathered

1. Terry C. Muck, "Questions about the Devotional Life," *Leadership* 3, no. 1 (Winter 1982): 31.
2. Phil Parshall, "How Spiritual Are the Missionaries?" *Evangelical Missions Quarterly* 23 (January 1987): 10-11.
3. James C. K. McClure, *Intercessory Prayer* (Atlanta: reprinted by Home Mission Board, SBC, 1987), p. 17.
4. Reported in *A Treasury of Prayer: The Best of E.M. Bounds on Prayer in a Single Volume*, compiled by Leonard Ravenhill (Minneapolis: Bethany House Publishers, 1981), p. 103.
5. Wesley L. Duewel, *Touch the World Through Prayer* (Grand Rapids: Francis Asbury Press, 1986), pp. 147-151.
6. Dick Eastman, *The Hour that Changes the World* (Grand Rapids: Baker Book House, 1978).
7. Muck, Ibid., p. 32.
8. Parshall, Ibid., pp. 10-11.

9. W. E. Sangster, "When I Find It Hard to Pray," *Classic Sermons on Prayer*, comp. Warren Wiersbe (Grand Rapids: Kregel Publications, 1987), pp. 155-156.

10. Lorne C. Sanny, "How to Spend a Day in Prayer" *Leadership*, (Summer 1982): 71-75. Also Lorne C. Sanny, *How to Spend a Day in Prayer* (Colorado Springs: Navpress, 1974), pp. 12-19.

6. The Lord's Prayer: Model Glue

1. Helmut Thielicke, *The Prayer That Spans the World* (E. T. London: James Clarke, 1960), p. 14.

2. Joel B. Green, Scot McKnight, and I. Howard Marshall, *Dictionary of Jesus and the Gospels* (Downers Grove: InterVarsity Press, 1992), p. 619.

3. William Barclay, *The Beatitudes and The Lord's Prayer for Everyman* (New York: Harper & Row, Publishers, 1924), pp. 175-76.

4. R. G. Lee, *A Charge to Keep* (Grand Rapids: Zondervan Publishing House, 1959), p. 105.

5. Karl Barth, *Prayer*, 2nd ed., by Don E. Saliers from the translation of Sara F. Terrien (Philadelphia: The Westminster Press, 1985), p. 59.

6. H. C. Morrison, "The Ladder of Prayer," *Classic Sermons on Prayer* by Warren Wiersbe (Grand Rapids: Kregel Publications, 1987), p. 149.

7. Theodore H. Robinson, *The Gospel of Matthew*, Moffatt's New Testament Commentary (New York: Harper & Row, n.d.), p. 51.

8. John R. W. Stott, *Confess Your Sins* (Philadelphia: Westminster Press, 1964), p. 73.

9. A. C. Dixon, "How to Pray," *Classics Sermons on Prayer* by Warren Wiersbe (Grand Rapids: Kregel Publications, 1987), p. 141.

10. James G. S. S. Thompson, *The Praying Christ* (Grand Rapids: Wm. B. Eerdmans Publishing Company, 1959), p. 96.

11. John R. W. Stott, "The Message of the Sermon on the Mount," (Matthew 5-7), *The Bible Speaks Today*, ed. John R. W. Stott (Downers Grove: InterVarsity Press, 1978), 151.

12. James Stewart, *Heralds of God* (New York: Charles Scribner's Sons, 1946), p. 90.

13. From a message delivered by Britt Towery, titled "The Evangelism that Works in China," November 6, 1990, Southwestern Baptist Theological Seminary, Fort Worth, Texas.

Part Two: The Prayer-Shaped Disciple Prays *Through*

1. This story was summarized in *Quote: The Speaker's Digest*, (February 1993): 58.

2. See also, *New Survey of Journalism* by George Fox Mott (New York: Barnes & Noble Books, 1953), p. 65 ff.

7. The Who Question: With a Little Help from My Friends

1. C.H. Spurgeon, "The Outpouring of the Holy Spirit," *The New Park Street Pulpit*, Vol. 4 (Pasadena, Texas: Pilgrim Publications, 1981), 296.

2. Prayer support letter from Glennda Cook, Taiwan, to Dan Crawford, Fort Worth, Texas, February 19, 1989.

8. The What Question: What's on Second

1. G. Campbell Morgan, *The Practice of Prayer* (New York: Fleming H. Revell, 1960), p. 111.

9. The Where Question: Does Location Matter?

1. S.D. Gordon, *Quiet Talks on Prayer* (Grand Rapids: Baker Book House, 1980), p.150.

2. Alan Walker, *Evangelistic Preaching* (Grand Rapids: Francis Asbury Press, 1988), p. 91.

3. "The Prayer: God knows now!" (Paul Harvey Products, Inc. distributed by Creators Syndicate, Inc., 1995).

4. Robert E. Coleman, *Songs of Heaven*, (Old Tappan, N.J.: Fleming H. Revell Company, 1980), p. 72.

5. Herbert Lockyer, *All the Prayers of the Bible*, (Grand Rapids: Zondervan Publishing House, 1959), p. 5.

10. The When Question: It's All in the Timing

1. John Baille, *A Diary of Private Prayer* (New York: Charles Scribner's Sons, 1949), p. 9.
2. Leonard Ravenhill, Comp. *A Treasury of Prayer: The Best of E.M. Bounds on Prayer* (Minneapolis: Bethany House Publishers, 1981), p. 100.
3. Lewis Gifford Parkhurst, Jr., *The Believer's Secret of Intercession: Compiled from the Writings of Andrew Murray and C.H. Spurgeon* (Minneapolis: Bethany House Publishers, 1988), p. 39.
4. R.C. Sproul, *Effective Prayer* (Wheaton: Tyndale House Publishers, 1987), p. 45.
5. John Lloyd Ogilvie, *Praying With Power* (Ventura, Calif.: Regal Books, 1983), p. 43.
6. Karl Barth, *Church Dogmatics: Index Volume with Aids for the Preacher*, ed. by G. W. Bromiley and T. F. Torrance (Edinburg: Clark, 1977), p. 414.
7. John Killinger, *Bread for the Wilderness, Wine for the Journey* (Waco: Word Books, 1976), p. 90.

11. The Why Question: A Child's Adult Question

1. James G. K. McClure, *Intercessory Prayer.* (Atlanta: Home Mission Board, SBC, 1987), pp.10–11.
2. Ibid, p. 14.

12. The How Question: When All Else Fails, Read the Instructions

1. D. L. Moody, *Prevailing Prayer* (Chicago: Moody Press, 1903), p. 93.
2. Bill Huebsch, *A New Look at Prayer* (Mystic, Conn.: Twenty-Third Publications, 1991), p. 2.

Part Three: The Prayer-Shaped Disciple Prays *Beyond*

13. Basic Ingredients—Mighty ACTS

1. Richard J. Foster, *Celebration of Discipline* (San Francisco: Harper San Francisco, 1978), p. 17.

2. Calvin Miller, *The Table of Inwardness* (Downers Grove: Inter-Varsity Press, 1984), p. 19.

3. E. M. Bounds, *Power Through Prayer* (Grand Rapids: Zondervan Publishing House, 1962), p. 66.

4. James Leo Garrett, Jr., "A Theology of Prayer," *Southwestern Journal of Theology*, (Spring, 1972): 4.

5. Reported in the "National and International Religion Report," (January 30, 1989) Vol. 3, No. 3: 8.

6. "Healing Power of Prayer Supported in Research Review," *Fort Worth Star-Telegram* (August 7, 1994).

7. For a fuller discussion of ways fasting adds to prayer, see *Mighty Prevailing Prayer* by Wesley Duewel (Grand Rapids: Francis Asbury Press, 1990), pp. 187-190.

8. Andrew Murray, *The Believer's School of Prayer* (Minneapolis: Bethany House Publishers, 1982), p. 77.

9. Richard Owen Roberts, *The Solemn Assembly* (Wheaton: International Awakening Press, 1989), p. 11.

10. Arthur Wallis, *God's Chosen Fast* (Fort Washington, Pa: Christian Literature Crusade, 1968), pp. 15-38.

11. O. Hallesby, *Prayer*, trans. by Clarence J. Clarsen (Minneapolis: Augsburg Publishing House, 1960), p. 113.

12. Andy Anderson, *Fasting Changed My Life* (Nashville: Broadman Press, 1977), p. 20.

13. Stormie Omartian, *Greater Health God's Way* (Chatsworth, Calif.: Sparrow Press, 1984), pp. 134-135.

14. Bill Bright, *The Coming Revival* (Orlando: New Life Publications, 1995), p. 126.

15. P.T. Forsyth, *The Soul of Prayer*, 5th ed. (London: Independent Press, 1966), p. 92.

14. Private to Public Prayer: Will You Lead Us?

1. Paul Y. Cho, *Prayer: Key to Revival* (Waco: Word Books, Inc., 1984), p. 102.
2. Lehman Strauss, *Sense and Nonsense about Prayer* (Chicago: Moody Press, 1974), pp. 9–10.
3. Theodore Jennings, "Prayer: The Call for God" *Christian Century* (April 15, 1981): 414.
4. George A. Buttrick, *Prayer* (New York/Nashville: Abingdon Press, 1942), p. 283.
5. LeRoy Patterson, "The Ten Most Unwanted Public Prayer Habits," *Eternity* (October 1982): 35–36.
6. Stanley J. Grenz, *Prayer: The Cry for the Kingdom* (Peabody, Mass.: Hendrickson Publishers, 1988), pp. 104–105.

15. For the Church: Body Language

1. *Webster's New World Dictionary*, 2nd College Ed., (1980), p. 82.
2. Ibid., p. 82.
3. *The Interpreter's Dictionary of the Bible* (Nashville: Abingdon Press, 1962), p. 399.
4. Richard Owen Roberts, "The Solemn Assembly" (Wheaton: International Awakening Press, 1989), p. 3.
5. Nels F. S. Ferre, *A Theology for Christian Prayer* (Nashville: Tidings, 1963), p. 9.
6. James M. Campbell, *The Place of Prayer in the Christian Religion* (New York: The Methodist Book Concern, 1915), p. 137.
7. Kenneth Scott Latourette, *A History of Christianity* (New York: Harper & Row Publishers, 1953), p. 203.
8. Dale Moody, *The Word of Truth* (Grand Rapids: Wm. B. Eerdmans Publishing Co., 1981), p. 158.
9. David Winter, *100 Days in the Arena* (Wheaton: Harold Shaw Publishers, 1977), Day 1.
10. Latourette, Ibid., p. 973.
11. Merrill E. Douglas and Joyce McNally, "How Ministers Use Their Time," *The Christian Ministry* (January 1980): 23.

12. C. Peter Wagner, *Prayer Shield* (Ventura, Calif.: Regal Books, 1992), p. 79.

13. John N. Vaughan, *The World's Twenty Largest Churches* (Grand Rapids: Baker Book House, 1984), p. 130.

14. Ibid., p. 66.

15. Ibid., p. 37.

16. George Barna, *User Friendly Churches* (Ventura, Calif.: Regal Books, 1991), p. 116.

17. See also George Barna, *User Friendly Churches* (Ventura, Calif.: Regal Books, 1991), Chapter 10, "You Do Not Have Because You Do Not Ask."

18. Elmer L. Towns, *An Inside Look at Ten of Today's Most Innovative Churches* (Ventura, Calif.: Regal Books, 1991), p. 22.

19. Ibid., p. 65.

20. Ibid., pp. 146-147.

21. "Does Prayer Make a Difference in Church Growth?" *Church Growth Today*, (Vol. 8, No. 5, 1993): 1-3.

22. Angela Chaffee, "The Tarahumara: Penetrating a People Through Prayer and Adoption," *Mission Frontiers Bulletin*, Vol. 16, No. 9-10 (Sept./Oct. 1994): 40-43.

23. Leonard Ravenhill, "No Wonder God Wonders," Great Commission Prayer League.

16. For Evangelism: As You Go ... Pray

1. *The International Bulletin of Missionary Research*, Vol. 16, No. 1 (January 1992): 27.

2. Stephen F. Olford, *Heart Cry for Revival* (Westwood, N.J.: Fleming H. Revell Company, 1962), p. 80.

3. John A. Abernathy, "The Shantung Revival," *The Church Proclaiming and Witnessing*, ed. Edwin L. McDonald (Grand Rapids: Baker Book House, 1966), pp. 81-83.

4. Lewis Drummond, *Miss Bertha: Woman of Revival* (Nashville: Broadman & Holman Publishers, 1996), pp. 45-46.

5. Paul Y. Cho, *Prayer: Key to Revival* (Waco: Word Books, Inc., 1984), p. 20.

6. John Avant, Malcolm McDow, and Alvin Reid, *Revival* (Nashville: Broadman & Holman, 1996), p. 176.
7. J.C. Ryle, *A Call to Prayer* (Grand Rapids: Baker Book House, 1976), pp. 14–15.

17. For World Missions: Praying to the Ends of the Earth

1. S. D. Gordon, *Quiet Talks on Prayer* (Old Tappan, N.J.: Fleming H. Revell Company, 1903), pp. 15, 82.
2. See also Francis McGaw, *Praying Hyde* (Minneapolis: Dimension Books, 1970).
3. Leonard Ravenhill, *Revival Praying* (Minneapolis: Bethany House Publishers, 1962), p. 123.
4. Lewis Drummond, *Miss Bertha: Woman of Revival* (Nashville: Broadman & Holman Publishers, 1996), p. 19
5. Alice Poyner, *From the Campus to the World* (Downers Grove: InterVarsity Press, 1986), pp. 111–112.
6. Quoted by Frank C. Laubach, "The Power of Intercession" in *Prayer: The Mightest Force in the World* (New York: Fleming H. Revell Co, 1946), p. 40.

18. Into Spiritual Warfare: Praying as to War

1. Roy C. Stedman, *Spiritual Warfare* (Portland: Multnomah Press, 1975), p. 130.
2. D. Martyn Lloyd-Jones, *The Christian Soldier* (Grand Rapids: Baker Book House, 1977), pp. 338–339.
3. As reported by Bob Vernon, Deputy Chief of Police, Los Angeles Police Department in "Illustration Digest" (Winslow, Arkansas: AA Publishing), April, 1992.
4. Walter Wink, *Naming the Powers* (Philadelphia: Fortress Press, 1984), p. 86.
5. C. Peter Wagner, *Warfare Prayer* (Ventura, Calif.: Regal Books, 1992), p. 53.
6. Mark I. Bubeck, *The Adversary* (Chicago: Moody Press, 1975), pp. 103–104.

7. Glen Martin and Dian Ginter, *Power House: A Step-By-Step Guide to Building a Church That Prays* (Nashville: Broadman & Holman Publishers, 1994), pp. 98–103.

Conclusion

1. E. F. and L. Harvey, *Kneeling We Triumph,* Book One (Hampton, Tenn: Harvey and Tait, 1982), p. 54.

Bibliography

Aldrich, Joe. *Prayer Summits.* Portland, OR: Multnomah Press, 1992.

Allen, Charles L. *All Things Are Possible through Prayer.* Westwood, NJ: Fleming H. Revell, 1957.

———. *Prayer Changes Things.* Westwood, NJ: Fleming H. Revell, 1964.

———. *Prayers that Changed History.* Nashville: Broadman Press, 1977.

Anderson, Andy. *Fasting Changed My Life.* Nashville: Broadman Press, 1977.

Andrew, Brother. *And God Changed His Mind.* Westwood, NJ: Fleming H. Revell, Chosen Books, 1990.

Anson, Elva. *How to Keep the Family that Prays Together from Falling Apart.* Chicago: Moody Press, 1975.

An Unknown Christian. *The Kneeling Christian.* Grand Rapids: Zondervan, 1971.

Archer, J. W. *Teach Us to Pray.* St. Louis: Concordia Publishing House, 1961.

Arthur, Kay. *Lord, Teach Me to Pray*. Eugene, OR: Harvest House Publishers, 1995.

Austin, Bill. *How to Get What You Pray For*. Wheaton, IL: Tyndale House, 1984.

Aycock, Don M. *Prayer 101*. Nashville: Broadman & Holman Publishers, 1998.

Bakke, Robert. *The Concert of Prayer: Back to the Future?* Minneapolis: Evangelical Free Church of America, 1992.

Barclay, William. *A Guide to Daily Prayer*. New York: Harper & Row Publishers, 1962.

Barry, James C. *Ideas for Effective Prayer Meetings*. Nashville: Convention Press, 1988.

Barth, Karl. *Prayer*. Translated by Sara F. Terrien. Philadelphia: Westminster Press, 1949.

Baughen, Michael. *Breaking the Prayer Barrier: Getting Through to God*. Wheaton: Harold Shaw Publishers, 1981.

Bauman, Edward J. *Intercessory Prayer*. Philadelphia: Westminster, 1958.

Beall, James Lee. *The Adventure of Fasting*. Westwood, NJ: Fleming H. Revell, 1974.

Bell, James S., Jr., ed. *Memos to God: A Prayer Journal Based on the Writings of E. M. Bounds*. Chicago: Moody Press, 1994.

Bevington, G. C. *Modern Miracles through Prayer and Faith*. Salem, OH: Schmul Publishing Co., n.d.

Bewes, Richard. *Talking About Prayer*. Downers Grove, IL: Inter-Varsity Press, 1979.

Biehl, Bob and J. Hagelganz. *Praying: How to Start and Keep Going*. Ventura, CA: Gospel Light, 1976.

Billheimer, Paul E. *Destined for the Throne*. Fort Washington, PA: Christian Literature Crusade, 1975.

Bisagno, John *The Power of Positive Praying*. Grand Rapids: Zondervan, 1965.

Blackaby, Henry T. and Claude V. King. *Faith Encounter: Experiencing God Through Prayer, Humility and Heartfelt Desire*. Nashville: Broadman & Holman, 1996.

Blackwood, Andrew W. *Leading in Public Prayer*. New York: Abingdon Press, 1958.

Blaiklock, E. M. *The Positive Power of Prayer*. Ventura, CA: Regal Books, 1974.

Bloesch, Donald G. *The Struggle of Prayer*. Colorado Springs: Helmers and Howard, 1988.

Bounds, E. M. *Power Through Prayer*. Grand Rapids: Baker Book House, 1972.

―――. *The Best of E. M. Bounds on Prayer*. Grand Rapids: Baker Book House, 1981.

Brane, Grace Adolphsen. *Receptive Prayer:A Christian Approach to Meditation*. St. Louis: CBP Press, 1985.

Bright, Bill. *The Coming Revival: God's Call to Fast, Pray and "Seek God's Face."* Orlando: New Life Publications, 1995.

Bright, Vonette and Ben A. Jennings. *Unleashing the Power of Prayer*. Chicago: Moody Press, 1989.

Brown, John. *An Exposition of Our Lord's Intercessory Prayer*. Grand Rapids: Baker Book House, 1980.

Brownson, William C. *Courage To Pray*. Grand Rapids: Baker Book House, 1989.

Bryant, David. *In the Gap*. Ventura, CA: Gospel Light/Regal Books, 1989.

―――. *Converts of Prayer*. Ventura, CA: Regal Books, 1988.

Burr, Richard A. *Developing Your Secret Closet of Prayer*. Camp Hill, PA: Christian Publications, 1998.

Buttick, George A. *So We Believe, So We Pray*. Nashville: Abingdon Press, 1951.

―――. *The Power of Prayer Today*. Waco, TX: Word Books, 1970.

Campbell, James M. *The Place of Prayer in the Christian Religion*. New York: Methodist Book Concern, 1915.

Carden, John, Comp. *A World at Prayer: The New Ecumenical Prayer Guide.* Mystic, CT: Twenty-Third Publications, 1990.

Carey, Walter J. *Prayer and Some of Its Difficulties*. London: A. R. Mowbray & Co., 1914.

Carse, James P. *The Silence of God*. New York: MacMillan, 1985.

Carson, D. A. *Teach Us to Pray: Prayer in the Bible and the World.* Grand Rapids: Baker Book House, 1989.

Carver, W.O. *Thou When Thou Prayest.* Nashville: Broadman Press, 1987.

Casteel, John L. *Rediscovering Prayer.* New York: Association Press, 1955.

Chadwick, Samuel. *The Path of Prayer.* London: Hodder and Stoughton, 1931.

Cho, Paul Y. *Prayer: Key to Revival.* Waco, TX: Word Books, 1984.

———.*Praying with Jesus.* Altamonte Springs, FL: Creation House, 1987.

Christenson, Evelyn and Viola Blake. *What Happens When Women Pray?* Wheaton: Victor Books, 1985.

Christenson, Evelyn. What Happens When God Answers. Waco: Word Publishers: 1986.

———.*What Happens When We Pray for Our Families.* Wheaton: Victor Books, 1992.

Clements, Ronald E. *In Spirit and in Trust: Insights from Biblical Prayers.* Atlanta: John Knox Press, 1985.

Coleman, Robert E. *Introducing the Prayer Cell.* Huntington Valley, PA: Christian Outreach, 1960.

Constable, Thomas S. *Talking to God.* Grand Rapids: Baker Books, 1995.

Cornwell, Judson. *The Secret of Personal Prayer.* Altamonte Springs, FL: Creation House, 1988.

Cove, Gordon. *Revival Now through Prayer and Fasting.* Salem, OH: Schmul Publishing Co., 1988.

Curran, Sue. *The Praying Church.* Lakeland, FL: Shekinah Publishing House, 1987.

Dawson, Joy. *Intercession, Thrilling and Fulfilling.* Seattle: YWAM Publishers, 1997.

Demaray, Donald E. *How Are You Praying?* Grand Rapids: Asbury Press, 1985.

———.*Alive to God Through Prayer.* Grand Rapids: Baker Book House, 1965.

Deweese, Charles W. *Prayer in Baptist Life.* Nashville: Broadman, 1986.

Dodd, M. E. *The Prayer Life of Jesus.* Wyckoff, NJ: Doran Co., 1923.

Donehoo, Paris. *Prayer in the Life of Jesus.* Nashville: Broadman Press, 1984.

Dood, Brian J. *Praying Jesus's Way*. Downers Grove: Inter-Varsity Press, 1997.

Drumwright, Huber L. *Prayer Rediscovered*. Nashville: Broadman Press, 1978.

Duewel, Wesley L. *Touch the World through Prayer*. Grand Rapids: Asbury Press, 1986.

———. *Mighty Prevailing Prayer*. Grand Rapids: Asbury Press, 1990.

Dunn, Ronald. *Don't Just Stand There, Pray* Something. Nashville: Thomas Nelson, 1991

Dunnam, Maxie. *The Workbook of Intercessory Prayer*. Nashville: The Upper Room, 1979.

———. *The Workbook of Living Prayer*. Nashville: The Upper Room, 1974.

Eastman, Dick. *A Celebration of Praise*. Grand Rapids: Baker Book House, 1984.

———. *Beyond Imagination*. Grand Rapids: Chosen Books, 1997.

———. *No Easy Road*. Grand Rapids: Baker Book House, 1971.

———. *The Hour That Changes the World*. Grand Rapids: Baker Book House, 1978.

———. *The Jericho Hour*. Orlando: Creation House, 1994.

———. *Love on Its Knees*. Grand Rapids: Chosen Books, 1989.

Eastman, Dick and Jack Hayford. *Living and Praying in Jesus' Name*. Wheaton: Tyndale House, 1991.

Eaton, Kenneth O. *Men On Their Knees*. New York: Abingdon Press, 1956.

Eims, Leroy. *Prayer: More than Words*. Colorado Springs: Navpress, 1984.

Elliff, Thomas D. *Praying for Others*. Nashville: Broadman, 1979.

———. *A Passion for Prayer*. Wheaton: Crossway Books, 1998.

Elliott, Norman. *How to Be the Lord's Prayer*. Waco: Word Books, 1968.

Erickson, Kenneth A. *Power of Praise*. St. Louis: Concordia, 1984

Ferre, Nels F. S. *A Theology for Christian Prayer*. Nashville: Nashville Tidings, 1963.

Finney, Charles G. *Prevailing Prayer*. Grand Rapids: Kregel Publications, 1965.

Finney, Charles G. *Principles of Prayer*. Minneapolis: Bethany House Publishers, 1980.

Fisher, Fred. *Prayer in the New Testament.* Philadelphia: Westminster Press, 1964.

Floyd, Ronnie W. *The Power of Prayer and Fasting.* Nashville: Broadman & Holman, 1997.

Forsyth, P. T. *The Soul of Prayer*. Grand Rapids: Eerdmans, 1960.

Fosdick, Harry Emerson. *The Meaning of Prayer.* New York: Association Press, 1915.

Foster, Richard J. *Celebration of Discipline.* San Fransciso: Harper Publishers, 1988.

———. *Prayer: Finding the Heart's True Home.* San Fransciso: Harper Publishers, 1992.

Freer, Harold Wiley and Francis B. Hall. *Two or Three Together.* New York: Harper & Row, 1954.

Frizzell, Gregory R. *Local Associations and United Prayer.* Memphis: Riverside Printing, 1996.

Fromer, Margaret and Sharrel Keyes. *Let's Pray Together.* Wheaton: Harold Shaw Publishers, 1974.

Gaddy, C. Weldon. *A Love Affair with God: Finding Freedom and Intimacy in Prayer.* Nashville: Broadman & Holman, 1995.

Getz, Gene A. *Praying for One Another.* Wheaton: Victor Books, 1988.

Goetsch, Ronald W. *Power through Prayer*. St. Louis: Concordia, 1959.

Gordon, S.D. *Quiet Talks on Prayer.* Westwood, NJ: Fleming H. Revell, 1904.

———. *Five Laws that Govern Prayer*. Westwood, NJ: Fleming H. Revell, 1925.

Grant, Peter. *The Power of Intercession.* Ann Arbor, MI: Servant Publications, 1984.

Grenz, Stanley J. Prayer: *The Cry for the Kingdom*. Peabody, MA: Hendrickson Publishers, 1988.

Griffin, Emilie. *Clinging: The Experience of Prayer.* New York: Harper & Row Publishers, 1984.

Guest, John. *Only a Prayer Away.* Ann Arbor, MI: Vine Books, 1985.

Gutzke, Manford. *Plain Talk on Prayer*. Grand Rapids: Baker Book House, 1973.

Haden, Ben. *Pray: Don't Settle for a Two-Bit Prayer Life*. Nashville: Thomas Nelson, 1974.

Hallesby, O. *Prayer.* Minneapolis: Augsburg Publishing House, 1934.

Hallock, E. F. *Always in Prayer*. Nashville: Broadman, 1966.

———. *Prayer and Meditation*. Nashville: Broadman Press, 1940.

Hamilton, Herbet Alfred. *Conversation with God: Learning to Pray*. New York: Abingdon Press, 1961.

Hanne, John Anthony. *Prayer or Pretense?* Grand Rapids: Zondervan Publishing House, 1975.

Harkness, Georgia. *Prayer and the Common Life*. New York: Abingdon-Cokesbury, 1948.

———. *How to Find Prayer More Meaningful*. Nashville: The Upper Room, 1946.

Harner, Philip B. *Understanding the Lord's Prayer.* Philadelphia: Fortress Press, 1975.

Harper, Steve. *Prayer Ministry in the Local Church*. Grand Rapids: Baker Book House, 1976.

Harries, Richard. *Prayer and the Pursuit of Happiness*. Grand Rapids: Eerdmans, 1985.

Harvey, E.F. and L.Harvey. *Kneeling We Triumph, Book One*. Hampton, TN: Harvey & Tait, 1982.

———. *Kneeling We Triumph, Book Two*. Hampton, TN: Harvey & Tait, 1992.

Hawkins, Frank. *The Church at Prayer*. Nashville: Broadman, 1986.

Hawthorne, Steve. *PrayerWalk Organizer Guide*. Austin, TX: Prayer Walk, USA, 1996.

Hawthorne, Steve and Graham Kendrick. *Prayerwalking*. Orlando: Creation House, 1992.

Hayford, Jack W. *Prayer Is Invading the Impossible*. Jacksonville, FL: Logos International, 1977.

Herman, Bridgid E. *Creative Prayer.* New York: Harper & Row Publishers, n.d.

Herring, Ralph A. *Cycle of Prayer*. Nashville: Broadman, 1966.

Hinson, E. Glenn. *The Reaffirmation of Prayer*. Nashville: Broadman, 1979.

Howington, Nelan P. *The Vigil of Prayer*. Nashville: Broadman Press, 1987.

Hubbard, David Allan. *The Practice of Prayer*. Downers Grove: Inter-Varsity Press, 1983.

Huebsch, Bill. *A New Look at Prayer*. Mystic, CT: Twenty-Third Publications, 1991.

Huegel, F. J. *The Ministry of Intercession*. Minneapolis: Bethany, Dimension Books, 1971.

Hughes, R. Kent. *Abba Father: The Lord's Pattern for Prayer.* Wheaton: Crossway Books, 1986.

Hulstrand, Donald. *The Praying Church.* New York: Seabury Press, 1977.

Humphries, Fisher. *The Heart of Prayer*. New Orleans: Insight Press, 1980.

Hunt, Art. *Praying with the One You Love.* Sisters, OR: Questar Publishers, Inc., 1996.

Hunt, T.W. *The Doctrine of Prayer*. Nashville: Convention Press, 1986.

———, Comp. *Church Prayer Ministry Manual*. Nashville: Baptist Sunday School Board, S. B. C., 1992.

Hunt, T. W. and Catherine Walker. *PrayerLife: Walking in Fellowship with God.* Nashville: Sunday School Board, S. B. C., 1987

Hunter, W. Bingham. *The God Who Hears*. Downers Grove: Inter-Varsity, 1986.

Hybels, Bill. *Too Busy Not to Pray.* Downers Grove: Inter-Varsity, 1988, 1998.

Jacobs, Cindy. *Possessing the Gates of the Enemy.* Grand Rapids: Chosen Books, 1991.

Jenkins, David L. *Great Prayers of the Bible*. Nashville: Broadman Press, 1990.

Jeremiah, David. *Prayer: The Great Adventure*. Sisters, OR: Multnomah Publishers, Inc., 1997.

Jeremias, Joachim. *The Lord's Prayer*. Translated by John Reumann. Philadelphia: Fortress Press, 1964.

Johnson, Ben Campbell. *To Pray God's Will.* Philadelphia: Westminster Press, 1987.

Johnstone, Patrick. *Operation World,* 5th ed. Grand Rapids: Zondervan Publishing House, 1993.

Jones, E. Stanley. *How to Pray.* Nashville: Abingdon Press, 1979.

Keating, Charles J. *Who We Are Is How We Pray.* Mystic, CT: Twenty-Third Publications, 1987.

Keller, W. Philip. *A Layman Looks at the Lord's Prayer.* Chicago: Moody Press, 1976.

Kelly, Douglas F. *If God Already Knows, Why Pray?* Brentwood, TN: Wolgemuth & Hyatt Publishers, 1989.

Killinger, John. *Bread for the Wilderness, Wine for the Journey: The Miracle of Prayer and Meditation.* Waco: Word Books, 1976.

Kimmel, Jo. *Steps to Prayer Power.* Nashville: Abingdon Press, 1972.

Kroll, Woodrow. *When God Doesn't Answer.* Grand Rapids: Baker Book House, 1997.

La Haye, Beverly. *Prayer: God's Comfort for Today.* Nashville: Thomas Nelson Publishers, 1990.

Laubach, Frank C. *Prayer: The Mightiest Force in the World.* Westwood, NJ: Fleming H. Revell, 1946.

Lavender, John Allen. *Why Prayers Are Unanswered.* Philadelphia: Judson Press, 1967.

Lawrence, Brother. *The Practice of the Presence of God.* Westwood, NJ: Fleming H. Revell, 1965.

Lawrence, R. *How to Pray when Life Hurts.* Downers Grove: InterVarsity Press, 1993.

Laymon, Charles M. *The Lord's Prayer.* Nashville: Abingdon Press, 1968.

Leach, Kenneth. *True Prayer.* New York: Harper and Row, 1980.

Lee, R. G. *The Bible and Prayer.* Nashville: Broadman Press, 1950.

Lewis, C. S. *Letters to Malcolm: Chiefly on Prayer.* New York: Harcourt, Brace, and World, 1964.

Lindsell, Harold. *When You Pray.* Grand Rapids: Baker Book House, 1969.

Lockyer, Herbert. *All the Prayers of the Bible.* Grand Rapids: Zondervan Publishing, 1959.

Lockyer, Herbert. *Power of Prayer*. Nashville: Thomas Nelson Pub., 1982.

Lord, Peter. *Hearing God*. Grand Rapids: Baker Book House, 1988.

Luthi, Walter. *The Lord's Prayer*. London: Oliver and Boyd, 1961.

MacArthur, John, Jr. *Jesus' Pattern of Prayer*. Chicago: Moody Press, 1981.

Macartney, Clarence Edward. *Wrestlers with God: Prayers of the Old Testament*. New York: R.R. Smith Inc., 1930.

MacDonald, Hope. *Discovering How to Pray*. Grand Rapids: Zondervan, 1976.

Maclachlan, Lewis. *Twenty-one Steps to Positive Prayer*. Philadelphia: Judson Press, 1978.

Magdalen, Margaret. *Jesus, Man of Prayer.* Downers Grove: Inter-Varsity Press, 1987.

Magee, John. *Reality and Prayer*. New York: Harper & Brothers, 1957.

Marshall, Catherine. *Adventures in Prayer*. Old Tappan, NJ: Chosen Books, 1975.

Martin, Glen and Dian Ginter. *Power House: A Step-by Step Guide to Building a Church that Prays*. Nashville: Broadman & Holman, 1994.

Martin, Linette. *Practical Praying.* Grand Rapids: Wm. B. Eerdmans Publishing Co., 1997.

Maxwell, John. *Partners in Prayer.* Nashville: Thomas Nelson Publishers, 1996.

McClure, James G. K. *Intercessory Prayer: A Mighty Means of Usefulness.* Chicago: Moody Press, 1902.

McDonald, H. D. *The God Who Responds*. Minneapolis: Bethany House, 1986.

McGaw, Francis. *Praying Hyde*. Minneapolis: Bethany Fellowship, 1970.

Metz, Johann and Karl Rahner. *The Courage to Pray*. Lexington Ave., N.Y.: Crossroad Publishing, 1981.

Miller, Calvin. *The Table of Inwardness*. Downers Grove: InterVarsity Press, 1984.

———. *Disarming the Darkness: A Guide to Spiritual Warfare*. Grand Rapids: Zondervan, 1998.

Moody, Dwight L. *Prevailing Prayer*. Chicago: Moody, 1962.

More, Hannah. *The Spirit of Prayer*. Grand Rapids: Zondervan, 1986.

Morgan, G. Campbell. *The Practice of Prayer*. Westwood, NJ: Fleming H. Revell, 1906.

Morrison, J. G. *The Stewardship of Fasting*. Kansas City, MO: Beacon Hill, n. d.

Morrissey, Kirkie. *On Holy Ground*. Colorado Springs: Navpress, 1983.

Mueller, George. *Answers to Prayer*. Chicago: Moody Press, 1895.

Murphy, Ed. *The Handbook for Spiritual Warfare*. Nashville: Thomas Nelson Publishers, 1992.

Murphy, Miriam. *Prayer in Action*. Nashville: Abingdon, 1979.

Murray, Andrew. *The Ministry of Intercessory Prayer*. Minneapolis: Bethany House, 1981.

———. *With Christ in the School of Prayer*. Westwood, NJ: Fleming H. Revell, 1985.

———. *The Believer's School of Prayer*. Minneapolis: Bethany House, 1982.

———. *The Prayer Life*. Springfield, PA: Whitaker House, 1981.

Myers, Warren and Ruth Myers. *Pray: How to Be Effective in Prayer*. Colorado Springs: Navpress, 1983.

———. *Praise: A Door to God's Presence*. Colorado Springs: Navpress, 1987.

Nee, Watchman. *The Prayer Ministry of the Church*. New York: Christian Fellowship Publishers, 1973.

———. *Let Us Pray*. New York: Christian Fellowship Publishing, 1977.

Ogilvie, Lloyd John. *Praying with Power*. Ventura, CA: Regal Books, 1983.

———. *Ask Him Anything*. Minneapolis: Grason, 1983.

———. *Conversation with God: Experience Intimacy with God through Personal Prayer*. Eugene, OR: Harvest House Publishers, 1993.

Orr, J. Edwin. *Fervent Prayer*. Chicago: Moody Press, 1974.

Palmer, B. M. *Theology of Prayer*. Harrisonburg, VA: Sprinkle Publications, 1980.

Parker, William R. and Elaine St. Johns. *Prayer Can Change Your Life*. Englewood Cliffs, NJ: Prentice-Hall, 1957.

Parkhurst, Louis Gifford, Jr. *Charles G. Finney's Principles of Prayer*. Minneapolis: Bethany Fellowship, 1980.

———, Comp. *The Believer's Secret of Intercession*. Minneapolis: Bethany House Publishers, 1988.

Parks, Helen Jean. *Holding the Ropes*. Nashville: Broadman Press, 1983.

Payne, Leanne. *Listening Prayer*. Grand Rapids: Baker Book House, 1994.

Peterson, Eugene H. *Earth and Altar: The Community of Prayer in a Self-Bound Society*. Downers Grove: Inter Varsity Press, 1985.

Pilkington, Evan. *Paths to Personal Prayer*. Mystic, CT: Twenty-Third Publications, 1990.

Poinsett, Brenda. *When Jesus Prayed*. Nashville: Broadman Press, 1981.

Prange, Edwin E. *A Time for Intercession*. Minneapolis: Bethany Fellowship, Inc., 1971.

Prince, Derek. *Shaping History through Prayer and Fasting*. Westwood, NJ: Fleming H. Revell, 1973.

Rainsford, Marcus. *Our Lord Prays for His Own: Thoughts on John 17*. Chicago: Moody Press, 1950.

Ravenhill, Leonard. *Revival Praying*. Minneapolis: Bethany House, 1962.

———, Comp. *A Treasury of Prayer: The Best of E.M. Bounds on Prayer in a Single Volume*. Minneapolis: Bethany House Publishers, 1981.

Redpath, Alan. *Victorious Praying*. Chicago: Moody Press, 1970.

Reidhead, Paris. *Beyond Petition*. Minneapolis: Bethany Fellowship, Inc., 1974.

Rhymes, Douglas. *Prayer in the Secular City*. Philadelphia: Westminster Press, 1967.

Rinker, Rosalind. *Communicating Love through Prayer*. Grand Rapids: Zondervan Books, 1969.

———. *Prayer: Conversing with God*. Grand Rapids: Zondervan Books, 1959.

———. *Praying Together*. Grand Rapids: Zondervan Books, 1968.

Roberts, Howard W. *Learning to Pray*. Nashville: Broadman Press, 1984.

Rodenmayer, Robert N. *The Pastor's Prayerbook*. New York: Oxford University Press, 1960.

Rossetti, Stephen. *I Am Awake: Discovering Prayer*. New York: Paulist Press, 1987.

Ryle, J. C. *A Call to Prayer*. Grand Rapids: Baker Book House, 1976.

Sanders, J. Oswald. *Prayer Power Unlimited*. Grand Rapids: Discovery House, 1977.

Sangster, W. E. *Teach Us to Pray*. London: Epworth, 1951.

Sangster, W. E. and Leslie Dawson. *The Pattern of Prayer*. Grand Rapids: Asbury Press, 1988.

Schaeffer, Edith. *The Life of Prayer*. Wheaton: Crossway Books, 1992.

Schuller, Robert H. *Prayer: My Soul's Adventure with God*. Nashville: Thomas Nelson Publishers, 1995.

Shedd, Charlie W. *How to Develop a Praying Church*. New York: Abingdon, 1964.

Sheets, Dutch. *Intercessory Prayer*. Ventura, Calif.: Regal Books, 1996.

Sherren, Quin. *How to Pray for Your Family*. Ann Arbor: Vine Books, 1990.

Sherren, Quin and Ruthanne Garlock. *The Spiritual Warrior's Prayer Guide*. Ann Arbor, MI: Servant Publications, 1992.

Shoemaker, Helen Smith. *The Secret of Effective Prayer*. Waco, TX: Word Publishers, 1967.

Silvoso, Ed. *That None Should Perish*. Ventura, CA: Regal Books, 1994.

Simpson, A. B. *The Life of Prayer*. Camp Hill, PA: Christian Publications, 1989.

Sims, A. *Mighty Prevailing Prayer*. Grand Rapids: Zondervan Publishing House, n.d.

Simundson, Daniel J. *Where Is God in My Praying?* Minneapolis: Augsburg Publishing House, 1986.

Smith, Alice. *Beyond the Veil*. Ventura, Calif.: Regal Books, 1997.

Smith, David R. *Fasting: A Neglected Discipline*. Fort Washington, PA: Christian Literature Crusade, 1993.

Smith, Eddie. *Help! I'm Married to an Intercessor*. Ventura, CA: Regal Books, 1998.

Spear, Wayne R. *The Theology of Prayer*. Grand Rapids: Baker Book House, 1979.

Sponheim, Paul R., ed. *A Primer on Prayer*. Philadelphia: Fortress Press, 1988.

Sproul, R. C. *Effective Prayer: Making Prayer All It Is Meant to Be.* Wheaton: Tyndale House, 1984.

Spurgeon, Charles H. *Effective Prayer*. N. P.: Evangelical Press, n.d.

Stanley, Charles F. *Handle with Prayer.* Wheaton: Victor Books, 1982.

———. *How to Listen to God*. Nashville: Thomas Nelson, 1985.

Stedman, Ray C. *Jesus Teaches on Prayer.* Waco, TX: Word Publishers, 1975.

———. *Talking to My Father*. Portland, OR: Multnomah Press, 1975.

———. *Spiritual Warfare.* Portland, OR: Multnomah Press, 1975.

Steere, Douglas V. *Dimensions of Prayer*. New York: Harper & Row, 1962.

Stewart, George S. *The Lower Levels of Prayer.* New York: Harper & Row, 1962.

Stokes, Mack B. *Talking with God*. Nashville: Abingdon Press, 1989.

Strauss, Lehman. *Sense and Nonsense about Prayer.* Chicago: Moody Press, 1974.

Strong, John Henry. *Jesus: The Man of Prayer*. Philadelphia: Judson Press, 1945.

Taylor, Jack R. *Prayer: Life's Limitless Reach*. Nashville: Broadman, 1977.

Thielicke, Helmut. *How We Learn to Speak with God*. Nashville: The Upper Room, 1973.

Thomson, James G. S. S. *The Praying Christ*. Grand Rapids: Eerdmans, 1959.

Toon, Peter. *From Mind To Heart: Christian Meditation Today.* Grand Rapids: Baker Book House.

———. *The Art of Meditating on Scripture*. Grand Rapids: Zondervan Publishing House, 1993.

Torrey, R. A. *The Power of Prayer*. Westwood, NJ: Fleming H. Revell, 1924.

———. *How to Pray.* Chicago: Moody Press, 1945.

Towns, Elmer. *Fasting for Spiritual Breakthrough*. Ventura, CA: Regal Books, 1996.

Trueblood, Elton. *The Lord's Prayer*. New York: Harper & Row, 1965.

Vander Griend, Alvin J. *The Praying Church Sourcebook*. Grand Rapids: Church Development Resources, 1990.

Verploegh, Harry., ed. *Oswald Chambers Prayer: A Holy Occupation*. Nashville: Discovery House Books, 1992.

Wagner, C. Peter. *Warfare Prayer*. Ventura, CA: Regal Books, 1992.

———. *Engaging the Enemy*. Ventura, CA: Regal Books, 1991.

Wagner, C. Peter, Stephen Peters and Mark Wilson. *Praying Through the 100 Gateway Cities of the 10/40 Window*. Seattle: YWAM Publishing, 1995.

Wallis, Arthur. *God's Chosen Fast*. Fort Washington, PA: Christian Literature Crusade, 1968.

———. *Jesus Prayed*. Fort Washington, PA: Christian Literature Crusade, 1966.

Weatherhead, Leslie D. *A Private House of Prayer*. New York: Abingdon Press, 1958.

Whiston, Charles Francis. *Pray: A Study of Distinctively Christian Praying*. Grand Rapids: Eerdmans, 1972.

———. *When Ye Pray Say Our Father*. Cleveland: Pilgrim Press, 1960.

White, John *Daring to Draw Near*. Downers Grove: InterVarsity Press, 1977.

White, Reginald E. O. *They Teach Us to Pray*. New York: Harper & Brothers, 1957.

White, Thomas B. *The Believer's Guide to Spiritual Warfare*. Ann Arbor, MI: Servant Publications, 1990.

Whitman, Virginia. *The Excitement of Answered Prayer*. Grand Rapids: Baker Book House, 1978.

Whittaker, Colin. *Seven Guides to Effective Prayer*. Minneapolis: Bethany House Publishers, 1987.

Whyte, Alexander. *Lord, Teach Us to Pray*. London: Hodder & Stoughton, 1922.

Wiersbe, Warren W., Comp. *Classic Sermons on Prayer*. Grand Rapids: Kregel Publications, 1987.

———. *Prayer: Basic Training*. Wheaton: Tyndale House, 1988.

Wiles, Gordon P. *Paul's Intercessory Prayers.* Cambridge: Cambridge University Press, 1974.

Williamson, Robert L. *Effective Public Prayer.* Nashville: Broadman Press, 1960.

Willis, Edward David. *Daring Prayer.* Atlanta: John Knox, 1977.

Winward, Stephen. *How to Talk to God.* Wheaton: Harold Shaw Publishers, 1973.